W9-DDQ-042

One Thousand Copies of

the First Edition of

BEAR ATTACK

by

Kathy Etling

have been printed by

SAFARI PRESS Inc.

This numbered and signed edition

is the Twelfth book in the

CLASSICS IN BIG-GAME HUNTING SERIES

This is copy number 759

Signed _____Kathy Etling_____
Kathy Etling

"Limited Edition"

This term has been used for about as long as there have been publishers. In recent years some publishers have discovered that if a limited edition is in great demand it pays to run extra copies to make more money. Unfortunately this practice has gotten out of hand, and some publishers print substantial amounts of extra copies above and beyond the stated limitation. These copies are then sold as "overruns" with the customer's name or reseller's name written where the number should be.

When we order our books from the printer, we never know exactly how many books we will receive. If we order 1,000 copies, we may receive anywhere from 950 to 1,050 copies. Also, it is necessary that we order a one- to two-percent overrun to compensate for books that are lost in the mail, damaged during transport, or sent out for review.

In order to guarantee our customers a truly limited edition of a book, we promise the following:

1. Safari Press will not issue more than a 5% overrun of any limited, numbered edition Safari Press book.

2. ALL review copies of our books will be stamped "Review: Not for resale" on the limitation page.

3. Should there be any copies left after all the numbers have been sold, the damaged and lost books have been replaced, and the review copies sent out, then these copies will be destroyed.

BEAR ATTACKS

BEAR ATTACKS

Classic Tales of Dangerous North American Bears

Kathy Etling

Volume I

Safari Press Inc.

P.O. Box 3095, Long Beach, CA 90803-0095, USA

Etling, Kathy

First Edition

1997, Long Beach, California.

ISBN 1-57157-047-0

Library of Congress Catalog Card Number: 96-69078

10 9 8 7 6 5 4 3 2 1

Readers wishing to receive the Safari Press catalog, featuring many fine books on big-game hunting, wingshooting, and sporting firearms, should write to Safari Press Inc., P.O. Box 3095, Long Beach, CA 90803, USA. Tel: (714) 894-9080, or visit our Web site at www.safaripress.com.

Table of Contents

Preface

Bears. The very word can send cold shivers up your spine or, at the very least, fan the flames of your imagination. Yet as a suburbanite who spent her life in the Midwest, I, like most other North Americans, had little or no contact with these majestic, fearful beasts.

That all changed, however, in 1988 when I reported for a long-awaited pack trip into Wyoming's remote Shoshone National Forest. For more than two weeks, my outfitter and I crisscrossed faint backcountry trails. Each day, we'd cut the tracks of grizzly bears seeking escape from the still-burning Yellowstone fires. We trekked through brooding conifers, across broad meadows, and into golden thickets of aspen, always pausing to scope out the next valley or ridgeline before moving on. When you're in bear country, you can never be too careful. My outfitter and I would often find fresh scat just outside our tents, as though hungry bears had lingered hopefully nearby, trying to figure out how to reach the treetop cache where we'd stored our food. At night, I'd listen to a chorus of sounds I could not recognize and wonder if out there, somewhere, lurked the bear that would amble through the wall of my tent.

About halfway through our trip, we decided to head for even rougher country. We asked another client to accompany us, both for the adventure and to help out with camp chores. He was a tall, hefty fellow, one who looked well suited to the task. He had a fun-loving personality, and was, quite frankly, the last person I would have imagined to be possessed of "bear-anoia."

That first night, I fell asleep slowly, thinking as always about the bears—both real and imagined—that could well be skulking just outside our tent flaps. Don—that was his name—fell asleep quickly, and was soon snoring loudly. Pure air and strenuous exercise finally did their parts, and I too fell sound asleep. When a bloodcurdling cry rent the air, I sat bolt upright in my sleeping bag.

"Help me, oh my God, help me!" Don screamed.

Dazed and confused in the interminable blackness, I reached for my gun. All I could think of was that a bear must have Don. I chambered a round, being careful to keep the safety engaged as I did so.

"Don! Are you okay?"

"Help me! Help me!" he cried out, sounding almost as though he was being smothered.

"What's wrong?" I asked. "Is it a bear?" I knew instinctively that if this were truly a bear attack, the animal would have already dragged Don into the forest. Still, I eased closer to his cot, just in case. More screams ensued. "Is it a bear?" I persisted. "Don . . . answer me. Is it a bear?"

By this time I was next to his cot, rifle in hand. The man was thrashing around, weeping, yet there was sheer terror in the occasional word he managed to utter.

"Don, I have a gun. If a bear has you, take the gun barrel and hold it against the animal and I'll shoot." Yet even as I spoke these words, I was fairly sure no bear was mauling Don.

"Where am I?" The words were soft and meek.

"You're in camp. Near Yellowstone. In Wyoming."

"Oh." Dead silence filled the darkness. "I must have had a bad dream."

I sighed, and my heart quit lurching about in my chest like a caged animal. "Go to sleep, Don."

"All right." Remarkably, in a few moments, the big man was snoring again. As though he was determined not to let me totally off the hook, Don started screaming once more that evening. This time, though, I was prepared. "Don, you're in Wyoming. You're in a spike camp. Go to sleep. You'll be okay." I know my voice sounded stern, but I couldn't help it. Finally, I heard his contented "okay" and then he dropped off to dreamland.

The mere suggestion of bears was all that it took to render this rugged individual into a glob of Silly Putty. And it's not that I see myself as being remarkably brave—after all, I did have a gun nearby. Don had left his outside (and that was probably for the good, suggestible as he was). He was screaming; I had to do something. I know I wasn't brave, for fear made it difficult to even push my breath out through my constricted chest.

Amazingly, the outfitter hadn't even been aware of the little drama that took place that night. The outfitter preferred sleeping beneath the stars, so he missed out on all the excitement. The next day, as the three of us rode high atop windswept ridges, I'd gaze at Don and remember his fear and think how incongruous it all seemed here in the warm, bright sunlight. And yet even as I thought it, I remembered my own terror, the way it had seeped through my bones and oozed from my pores, and I thought of all the other people who live and work and play every day in bear country. I wondered what it was like to actually be attacked by a bear, and I wondered what the chances were of it happening. What's more, I wondered if there was anything people could do to help to prevent such attacks or, should one occur, to lessen its severity.

I understood, viscerally, the vital role that bears play in our lives. To both city-dwellers and rural folk, bears are an integral part of our last remaining wilderness areas. Bears are mysterious. They are often huge, and, under the right circumstances, they can be ferocious. They have shared this earth with us for eons, and their very presence affects us in ways that we—technologically advanced as we may be—cannot even begin to understand. They are part of our heritage as humans. They are cohabitants of our earth and as such, are worthy of our respect. But strangely enough, the very topic of bears has become a battleground.

Some people malign bears. Some deify bears. Of those who malign them, a few—if able to—would trap or shoot or kill every last bear on this earth. Those who deify them are fond of carping at the rest of us that "bears were here first." This group fights daily skirmishes aimed at not only eliminating all people from bear habitat, but also halting any and all harassment of bears, be it by hikers, horseback riders, or hunters.

Between these two extremes lies the vast majority of the rest of us, people who neither malign nor deify bears. But people of today, however good their intentions, labor under a tremendous burden of misperception and misinformation. And that's why I wrote this book. I would like to entertain you with classic tales of some of the most exciting North American bear attacks of all time. These are thrilling tales, but my purpose in relating them here isn't to scare you. No, in telling or retelling these stories, I hope not only to entertain you but also to teach you a little bit about bears. For bears are an integral part of our past and, with any luck, will be a vital part of our future. In most cases, bears act in predictable ways. If we know—or can predict—what a bear will do, we can actually lessen the danger when venturing into bear country.

I envisioned these two volumes as much more than just a rehashing of thrilling North American bear tales. Volume I will take you back to the dim beginnings when early humans vied with ancient bears in a never ending quest for food and shelter. In this first book we will examine the role bears played in shaping what we humans eventually became, and how they influenced the way we see the world around us. We will look into the worlds of art and literature to examine the legends and myths of our forefathers that once elevated bears to the level of our own human race. We will be there with the Native Americans, the explorers, the mountain men, and the ranchers as they encounter these awesome creatures. We will see how conflict with bears shaped the North American experience, and how it continues to do so today.

In Volume II we will begin to piece together the bear puzzle confronted by these earliest Americans. We, from our modern-day perspective, will examine theories of bear evolution to try to understand why these animals behave the way they do. We will consider bear biology and how adaptations have allowed this animal to keep pace with its rapidly changing world. We will read the tales of some of the most horrible bear attacks of all time. Finally, we will receive expert advice on how to remain unharmed when visiting bear country.

Along the way, we will see how bears have stirred the embers of our souls from time immemorial—and how they stir us still—in ways we modern people, snug in our safe, all-weather homes, can hardly imagine.

Acknowledgments

Writing this book would have been far more difficult without help from a great many people. Since I am a writer and a reporter, not a bear biologist, behaviorist, or paleontologist, advice and comments from noted authorities in these fields were invaluable while piecing together the chapters of this book. I'm especially grateful to David Mattson of the University of Idaho for his help in editing the chapters on bear evolution and behavior; to Kevin Frey of the Montana Division of Fish, Wildlife and Parks for the long hours spent poring over the black bear and grizzly bear biology chapters, as well as the chapters on attack prevention; and to Scott Schliebe of the U.S. Fish and Wildlife Service's Marine Mammal Management Office for doing the same for the chapters on polar bears.

During my research, I contacted biologists all over North America. Many of them provided specific information, leads to recent or obscure attacks, moral support, and lots of encouragement. Chief among them are Dave Hamilton of the Missouri Department of Conservation; Harry Jacobson of the Mississippi Cooperative Wildlife Research Unit; Bob Stafford of the California Department of Fish and Game; Tom Beck, Nick Pinnell, and Willy Travnicek, all of the Colorado Division of Wildlife; Mark Bruscino, Dave Moody, and Tom Thorne, all of the Wyoming Game and Fish Department; Kerry Gunther and Mark Biel of the Yellowstone National Park Bear Management Office; Gary Alt of the Pennsylvania Game Commission; Boyd

Blackwell of the Utah Division of Wildlife Resources; Darrell Weybright and Cicely Costello of the New Mexico Department of Game and Fish; Lou Berchielli of the New York Department of Environmental Conservation; John Wooding of the Florida Game and Freshwater Fish Commission; Dick Sellers, Matt Robus, and Dick Shideler of the Alaska Department of Fish and Game; Steve Shively of the Louisiana Natural Heritage Program; Hilary Meier of Denali National Park; Chris Servheen of the U.S. Fish and Wildlife Service; Randy Seguin of the Saskatchewan Office of Environment and Resource Management; Hank Hristienko of the Manitoba Department of Natural Resources; John Gunson of the Alberta Natural Resources Service; Sean Sharpe of the Wildlife Branch of British Columbia's Ministry of the Environment; Bob Hofman of the Marine Mammal Commission; and Bill Alther of the Denver Museum of Natural History.

I also owe a debt of gratitude to researcher and grizzly bear legend Frank Craighead, as well as to attack victims Cynthia Dusel-Bacon, George and Krystal Gadd, Howard and Norma Haymond, Mattie Jack, Marti Miller, Don Chaffin, Jim Craig, Roy Ducat, Marlin Grasser, Mark Matheny, Bert O'Connell, Fred Treul, and Ed Wiseman for allowing me to tell their stories. Special thanks are also due Albert McClelland for granting me permission to use the moving letter he wrote to his late son, Colin.

Finally, I would like to thank David E. Browne; Brad Garfield, the editor of "Bears" magazine, which is published in Tremonton, Utah; renowned bear outfitters Dennis Harms and Jim Shockey; Becky Shay; Bob Robb; and, last but not least, Russ Thornberry for also helping out in innumerable ways during the time I was researching this book.

Kathy Etling

Dedication

To my husband, Bob.

PART

North American Bears

I

1

The Bear Within

There is a bear within each one of us. It lurks inside our minds and permeates our souls. In some of us, the bear slumbers quietly, and if we're aware of its existence at all, it is but vaguely. In others, the bear prowls restlessly, barely restrained beneath a deceptively calm exterior, a living, breathing personification that's an integral part of who and what we are. The bear within differs only in degree. But each individual who pays close attention to bears, observes their actions with truly open eyes, or reads to unlock the secrets of their existence can sense the bond shared by our two species. This has been true since our ancestors first pulled themselves upright and became, for a long period, opportunistic foragers like the bears. It will remain true until the end of time, or until the last bear is forever gone.

Our ancestors looked to the bears for the keys to their survival. They attempted to glean from the wise old grandfathers of the forests answers to questions not completely understood. *Homo sapiens sapiens* evolved independently of the great bears, yet we share with them a commonality, a duality, of life and of living so deep and intense that many modern people, though distanced from the wilderness, remain firmly in their thrall. It's as though that spark of kinship still smolders, while a primeval need urges us—perhaps on a subliminal plane—to learn more about animals essentially unchanged from the time we humans crawled out of the trees.

Modern humans stand alone at the top of the food chain, a position attained only recently. To get there, we had to displace animals much stronger and faster than ourselves, animals like the bears. We pushed and we shoved, and by dint of our intellectual superiority and an utterly ruthless desire to conquer all we surveyed, we finally knocked them down and—in many places—all but out. We prevailed, but something strange happened as we stood poised to finish them off altogether. For a brief second in time, after having eliminated them from much of their former range, we hesitated. Perhaps we recognized that in destroying the bears and the wilderness that sheltered them, we would be destroying something of ourselves: the bear within us all. Our mandate shifted. We began to study these creatures, and in the process we learned they are far more like ourselves than some of us might care to admit. For we, like the great bears, have survived by adapting to a rapidly changing world. We, like the bears, are opportunists. We share with them a high degree of intelligence, an upright stance (occasional, in the case of the bear), stereoscopic vision, dexterous hands and paws, an innate curiosity, a predator's instincts, and the fierceness and willingness to defend what is ours.

While it has taken us humans perhaps 2 million years to evolve, the bear has been changing slowly for at least 40 million. Bears continue to evolve even today, in marked contrast to humankind, in which some scientists believe the evolutionary processes may be stalled. Given our propensity to meddle—or to save those of our species who would not live without medical assistance, mechanical aids, or someone else's willingness to obtain food and shelter for them at a price—today's humans are, alone among the animals, truly equal among each other. And if humans are not born equal, then we will surely *make* them equal. But out of that enforced equality will come no new adaptations favoring some individuals and not others. So for all intents and purposes, the argument goes, human evolution has ceased.

But the great bears continue trundling down that rocky road so recently abandoned by our own kind. Bears, unlike humans, still depend upon only themselves for their survival and, for perhaps two or three early years, their mothers. So evolution continues—and may even be accelerating—as external pressures mount. For bears are in a fight for their lives, a fight waged against them by those humans who still do not understand them and who do not care to understand them. If bears do survive far into the future, it will be only the strongest and most adaptable among them that will do so.

Our ancestors must surely have gazed upon the great bears with awe. What were these giant beasts who could smite feeble humanity into oblivion with but a flick of one paw? Were bears simply a stronger, far superior race of humans? That would not have been such a farfetched conclusion for them to have reached. After all, when skinned, a bear's body resembles a man's. They walk erect, love their children, and even prepare shelters in which to spend cold weather.

Siegfried Giedion, writing in *The Eternal Present: The Beginnings of Art*, came to the conclusion that early humans believed they were intrinsically inferior to the animals. Giedion thought that since they relied on animal protein to survive, they must have felt as though they occupied a much lower rung on the overall hierarchical ladder. Early humans surely realized that they were far less powerful than mammoths, lions, or bears. They understood that without animals, they would die. Early men owed animals a tremendous debt. Each glimpse of a living creature reminded our primitive ancestors that their own lives depended on the killing and devouring of other, more sacred beings.

Over time primitive men gradually amended that idea. They came to the conclusion that humans were brothers and sisters with animals, a definite step up in the ranks. Totemism developed as humans divined a spiritual kinship with those animals most revered for cunning, speed, or strength. Tales were told and retold, one generation to the next, in which an animal became human or a human took on an animal's form. These tales served to prove the special relationship between humans and animals. And through the ages, perhaps no greater bond was ever forged than the one linking humans and bears.

Archaeologists who excavated a cave in Drachenloch, Switzerland, discovered ancient altars dating from 75,000 B.C. or even earlier constructed "for the ritual of the bear," as well-known author and mythologist Joseph Campbell described it. Although no one is positive that bear rituals actually took place, cave bear skulls were strategically placed within the cave's innermost recesses. Only human beings could have positioned them so deliberately.

In Regordou, France, a brown bear's body was buried in a trench and then covered with a large gravestone. Some scientists theorize that this was how Neanderthal humans paid homage to the spirit of the bear. In Bavaria's Petershohle Cave, ten bear skulls were stacked high atop a platform. The immense amount of work involved proves how important bears must have been to early humans.

Bears are a part of who we are. Many of us probably owe our very existence to an ancestor who huddled in a bearskin or survived lean times by subsisting on bear meat. The development of language illustrates the influence of these animals. The Teutonic stem word *ber* was the forerunner of *bar*, the German word for bear. Proper names like Bernard, Bertha, and Robert are derived from the word for bear, and Bjorn itself is Scandinavian for bear.

The Greek word for bear is *arctos*, and from this we arrive at Arctic, a region in which great bears thrive. *Arctos* is also the root of Arthur, a legendary King of England rumored to be sleeping (like a hibernating bear?) on the island of Avalon.

We store hay over the winter in a barn much as the bear stores himself in a den. We lay the bodies of the dead on a bier hoping that they, like the dormant bear, will one day be resurrected. A barrow moves heavily across the ground, lumbering to its destination like a bear. Beer is made from barley, the bear's grain because it was once fermented underground. We bury our dead and burrow under the ground. The word brown comes from the German *bruin*, which is simply another word for bear.

We bear or endure our troubles or burdens. Women bear children after many months, which are analogous to a bear's hibernation. We take bearings when we travel to reach our destination, hoping that, like the bear, we will arrive with a minimum of trouble.

The concept of bearings deserves a closer examination and so we look to the sky to gaze at constellations such as Ursa Major and Ursa Minor: the Big Bear and the Little Bear. Many ancient people of the Northern Hemisphere associated these star groupings with bears. When they used the sky to navigate, they got their bearings by using the brightest star in the Little Bear, Alpha Ursae Minoris, also known as Polaris, or the North Star.

The Greeks had their own legend explaining the origins of these two groups of stars. Once upon a time, the god Jupiter fell in love with Callisto, a beautiful nymph. Callisto bore a son from the union and he was named Arcas. One day, Jupiter's wife, Juno, discovered the lovers. She became so jealous she turned Callisto into a bear. Shunned by the other animals and hunted by men, Callisto had a hard time of it in the forest. One day, after several years, she saw her son, Arcas. She wanted to get close to the young man, but since she was a bear, he did not recognize his own mother. He was about to hurl his spear at Callisto when Jupiter intervened. The god saved Callisto's life by turning Arcas into a bear. He then placed both mother and son in the northern sky where you can still see them today.

The people who first saw images of bears in the sky probably walked the earth during the time of *Ursus spelaeus*, the cave bear, since, like the cave bear, both Ursa Major and Ursa Minor possess long tails. The Greeks, who lived well after the last cave bear had disappeared from the earth, neatly explained the constellations' tails by saying that when Jupiter heaved the two bears far into the heavens, their once-stubby tails stretched.

The constellation Boötes, the Bear Keeper or Bear Hunter, remains at the heels of the two bears. Arcturus, the brightest star in Boötes, gets its name from the Greek: *arctos* for bear, and *ouros* for keeper.

The Indians of North America were well aware that bears didn't have long tails. In their mythology they described the three stars (regarded by their European counterparts as the bears' tails) as hunters chasing two bears through the sky for all eternity. In autumn, as the Big Bear and the Little Bear dipped close to the horizon, the Native Americans agreed that the bears were simply seeking a safe place where they might sleep the winter away.

By the time of the world's first art, man probably believed that everything within the natural world possessed a soul. This included the animals, and most certainly the bears, for of all the creatures of the Northern Hemisphere, bears were most like himself. In Montespan, France, a rough model of a headless bear measuring almost three feet in length was discovered secreted in a cave. An actual bear's skull was found lying between the sculpture's forelegs. Perhaps early humans once fastened it to the body by a wooden peg. One can imagine Cro-Magnon men draping a bearskin upon the sculpture, completing the illusion. Other statues elsewhere have been found riddled with holes, perhaps from ritual spears that were once thrown at them.

Most haunting of all are the cave paintings, the silent yet reverent depictions of animals created upon rock walls deep within the bowels of the earth during the latter half of the last ice age. These paintings almost certainly served as a part of some religious rite or ritual. Many animals are represented, but only a few are bears. Perhaps the spirit of the bear was considered far too powerful—and too sacred—to be trifled with by mere humanity. And, perhaps, that is as it should be.

PART

Early Grizzly
Attacks

II

2

Myth of the Grizzly

From time immemorial the North American Indians have dwelled in a world populated by spirits. It mattered not whether a tribe of The People inhabited the coastal plains or the Great Plains—they all regarded birds as messengers to the gods, rocks as possessing souls, and animals like the bears as a very big source of medicine indeed. Their world was filled with spirits, some good and some evil, but all had to be placated if lowly humans were to thrive upon this earth. The roots of these beliefs reach back through hundreds of thousands of years. They extend beyond Beringia to the land from which The People came, and within their oral traditions are stories similar to those told in the Bible.

According to Indian legend, animals helped the Great Spirit create humans. Animals then served as mentors to humans, revealing to them all the mysteries of the natural world. But The People soon grew proud. They grew arrogant. They commanded the beaver to fell logs for their canoes and robbed the wild bees for their honey. The animals grew tired of such treatment and finally abandoned The People, refusing to ever speak their language again.

Although a rift had developed between humans and animals, a bond remained. To early Native Americans, humans and animals were more alike than different. They believed both groups had souls, and that whenever animals desired, they could transform themselves into human form. And when animals became human, it was to share their secrets so The People could survive.

"We know what the animals do, what are the needs of the beaver, the bear, the salmon, and other creatures, because long ago men married them and acquired this knowledge from their animal wives," explained an Athapaskan hunter of the early twentieth century. "The white man has been only a short time in this country and knows very little about the animals. We have been here thousands of years and were taught long ago by the animals themselves."

With such a philosophy, no wonder the Indians showed such great respect for animals. Although they hunted, their hunting rituals exhibited a profound moral code, one formulated back in the days when animals could speak to humans and tell them what they desired. And the moral code governing the treatment of bears was stricter than for any other animal. The Indians were well aware how much bears resemble people. They stand erect and can even walk upright for a short distance. Bears can reach with their paws, pick berries, and sit on their haunches. Their eyes are placed on the fronts of their heads, and as they move slowly across the earth, they appear to give a great deal of consideration to tasks such as digging up mice and excavating dens. Indians believed that bears know many secrets. They know which plants can be used for healing, which roots provide sustenance, and where the best berries are found. They even line their winter dens with evergreen boughs. How much more like a human can an animal be?

With so many similarities, it's no wonder Indians believed that bears would often assume human form. Several tribes tell the tale of Bear Woman, a bear who became human to marry an unsuspecting warrior. Eventually, she reverted to her bear form, but not before she'd revealed to her husband everything he needed to become a great bear hunter. What she told him enabled The People to survive lean years from that time on. The debt they owed the bears for this great gift was tremendous.

Another tale, this one from the Haida tribe of British Columbia and related in Sanders & Shephards's *The Sacred Paw*, told a different version of the bond linking humans with bears.

❖   ❖   ❖

One day, long ago, a group of girls was out gathering berries. One girl was a chatterbox. She should have been singing to let the bears know she was near, instead of talking and laughing. The bears, who heard her babbling from a long distance, wondered if she was mocking with all her foolish words. By the time the girls were through picking berries, the bears had moved close so they could watch them.

The talkative girl followed the rest of the girls down the trail toward home. But as she walked she stepped in some bear dung and slipped. When she slipped, the strap that held the pack filled with berries to her back broke. Instead of crying out, she spoke angrily and complained. The bears, who were still watching, spoke of this. "Does she speak of us like this?" one asked.

It was now growing dark. Two young men who looked like brothers appeared from the shadows and approached the girl. One said "Come with us. We will help carry your berries." As the young woman followed the men she noticed that they were wearing bear robes.

It was dark when they finally arrived at a house near a rock slide high above timberline. Inside the house were many people, all of them wearing bearskins. Grandmother Mouse ran up to the girl and squeaked that she had been taken into a bear den and was soon to become one of them. The girl became frightened. She looked at her robe and noticed that the hair on it was already growing longer and more like a bear's. One of the young bears came to her and said, "You will live if you become my wife. Otherwise, you will die."

She had no choice. She became the bear's wife. She tended their fire and saw that whenever the Bear People went outside they would put on their bear coats and become like the animal. That winter she became pregnant. Her husband took her to a cave where she gave birth to twins, which were half human and half bear.

One day her brothers came searching for her. The Bear Wife saw them and rolled a snowball down the mountainside to get their attention. They climbed the hill to meet her and saw the Bear Husband. The Bear Husband knew then that he must die. Before his wife's brothers killed him, he taught her and his Bear Sons the songs the hunters must sing over his dead body to ensure their continued good fortune. He willed his skin to his wife's father, the tribal chief. The young men killed the bear, smoking him out of the cave and spearing him. They took the two children and their sister, the Bear Wife, back to her own people.

The Bear Sons removed their bear coats. They became great and honored hunters, guiding their kinsmen to many dens. They showed them how to set snares and how to sing the ritual songs. And when their mother died many years later, they once again put on their bear coats and returned to live with the Bear People. But because of what they had showed their kinsmen, the tribe continued to have good hunting.

The People lived in harmony with the earth. As anthropologist and ethnologist Richard Nelson wrote, "The Koyukon Indians move with their surroundings, not attempting to control, master, or fundamentally alter them. They do not confront nature, they yield to it."

Native Americans could look to the bear as an example of how to exist in peaceful harmony with their surroundings. Like the bear, they would not fight but yield to the overpowering forces of nature. When the winter sun appeared to be deserting the earth, The People would, like the bear, hole up until it returned. Indians knew springtime had finally arrived when the bear moved from its den. Often, the bear would be leading a new brood, providing a living symbol of the rebirth of the earth and the hope of immortality. Bears, which disappeared without a trace each fall only to appear anew in the spring, were the very embodiment of the concept of life after death.

Bears not only personified life to these early people, the flesh of their bodies literally bestowed upon them life itself. In the early nineteenth century, mountain men spoke of "rabbit starvation," the withering loss of flesh that resulted from a lack of fat in the diet. To those who lived off the earth, fat was more valuable than gold. And no animal provided more of the rich, life-giving substance than the bear. When a bear was killed, nothing was wasted. Its fat was rendered and produced gallons of sweet-smelling bear oil. The meat was roasted, boiled, or dried. The hide was scraped and tanned and used for robes or blankets. Its bladder and stomach were saved as storage vessels. Tendons and sinew were stripped and dried for use in sewing. And the bear's teeth and claws, the very essence of its medicine, were claimed by the strongest warrior or the most potent shaman.

But to properly retrieve these gifts from the bear required painstaking rites and rituals. In the book *Northern Tales*, John Rains, a Cree Indian, states: "Animals expect us to act properly. We can't cause them any suffering. That's why we have to teach our sons to shoot well, so that animals don't suffer. If we behave badly toward animals they leave."

Some tribes demonstrated their respect to the bears in other ways. Warriors of the Northwest Indian tribes would often fast and abstain from sexual intercourse before hunting the grizzly. In many societies, once a kill had been made the bear's head and skin would be positioned exactly as though the animal were a tribal chief, lying in state. They would paint the bear's head with sacred red ochre, and perhaps decorate it with eagle down. Bones were handled reverently for two reasons: first, so that the bear might return again; and second, so that the dead bear's friends would not wreak vengeance upon the hunter.

The Indians would then offer prayers of thanksgiving to the slain animal, concluding the ritual by asking the bear to tell its Spirit Keeper that it had been well treated. Native Americans believed that if a bear was so honored, more bears would offer themselves up to be killed. One such prayer to the bear belonged to the Kwakiutl, a Northwest tribe, and went like this:

You will be known all over the world, as far as the edge of the world, you Great One who safely returned from the spirits.

Bears meant many things to the early natives. Their "medicine" varied depending on the beliefs of the tribe. Among the Sioux, the bear was considered the most potent source of strength in nature. Warriors invoked the bear's spirit before heading into battle. They painted marks on their bodies that resembled scratches from claws and carried knives with handles carved from bear jawbones. Some warriors wore bear claws and teeth and painted bears on war shields and war ponies. Shamans from tribes as diverse as the Sioux, Pueblo, and Chippewa would sometimes dress as bears when healing the sick. They believed that the bear was so powerful, it could overpower almost any evil spirit within the sick person's body.

When Assiniboin warriors recited their deeds of war, they included all the bears they had ever killed. The Fox scalped dead bears as proof of their fearlessness in battle. The Wintun and Nomlaki used grizzly bear pelts as shrouds for their dead. When they carefully wrapped a body with the fur facing inward to touch the skin of the corpse, they perhaps hoped to confer the bear's immortality upon the deceased.

Although the Kutenai regarded the Sun Dance as their most important religious ceremony, the Grizzly Bear Dance was not far behind. If the Grizzly Bear Spirit was properly impressed by the prayers of The People, he would lead them to the best berries. In eastern portions of the Great Basin, Bear Dance participants were blessed with both hunting and sexual prowess.

Yosemite National Park owes its very name to the great grizzly bear, "Uzumati," that once inhabited its landscape. According to legend, a young chief was on his way to Mirror Lake when a huge grizzly confronted him. The bear attacked the chief, who carried no weapon. The grizzly was relentless, and it fiercely mauled the young chief, who looked around desperately before arming himself with a dead tree limb. Bleeding from many wounds, the man finally killed the bear. When he returned to his tribe, they changed his name to that of the mighty grizzly, Uzumati, or Yosemite.

While all tribes looked upon the grizzly or brown bear with awe and respect, some were so fearful of its power that they refused to meddle with something so potent. The Apache, for instance, were well aware that honoring the bear's spirit could bring blessings to the tribe. But they tempered this knowledge with the fear that provoking the bear might bring harm. That is why the Apache forbade the killing of bears. Tribal elders would not even allow their people to touch a dead bear that had been found in the woods.

The Sierra Miwok of California believed that when spirits of malevolent shamans returned to the earth they appeared in the form of grizzly bears. Mindful of what these evil shamans might do, these people took great pains to avoid the animal.

After slaying a bear, some northern Athapaskan tribes would cut off its forepaws and poke out its eyes so the dead animal could neither see who had killed it nor hunt them down.

The specter of imminent attack was very much a part of the early Native American's daily life. The Chugach Eskimo considered the hostility of local brown bears to be related to a shunned bear wife's retribution. According to their legend, a man left his bear wife to go hunting and never returned. At first she mourned him because she thought he was dead. But later, a bird told her that her husband still lived. Overcome with joy, she set out to see if this was true. But when she discovered her husband alive and living with two women, she became enraged. She waited until her husband went away and then turned herself into a bear and killed the two women. She then lay in wait for her husband. When he returned, she killed him too.

The Kutenai, who lived in an area of grizzly bear abundance, performed a dance that honored the bears before they emerged from hibernation. The Kutenai felt if they properly honored the bears, they would be secure from attack the following year.

California's Pomo Indians explained bear attacks quite differently. They believed evil "bear doctors" would dress up like grizzlies to kill unsuspecting tribesmen for their goods and food. Because their fear of grizzlies, or bear doctors, was so great, the Pomo would not allow their young men to hunt alone until they were twenty-five or thirty years of age.

The legend of these "bear men," or *gauk buraghal*, persists to this day. California tribes like the Patwin, Maidu, and Pomo all believed they existed. Supposedly, the bear men were allowed to murder four tribesmen each year. While wearing a bearskin, an evil shaman would surprise his victim, attacking fiercely like a grizzly bear, and use a knife to first scratch out his victim's eyes. Then he would stab his victim to death, holding his knife as though it were teeth or claws. Once the victim was dead, the bear man would rip open his stomach, disembowel him, then scatter the remains over the ground, just as an enraged bear might do.

Real grizzlies must have exacted a terrible toll on California Indians. Whenever one of these Indians passed a place where a bear had once killed someone, he would toss a stone or pebble upon the spot. Through the years, great mounds of stone were amassed in various places, warning all who passed that a grizzly might be near.

The Wailaki, another California tribe, would hang any dead bear's hide outside their sweathouse where members of the tribe could beat upon it with their fists. They would work themselves into a frenzy as they pummeled the bear hide for days on end.

Most Native Americans regarded the bear with great respect. All regarded it with awe. A very few took every opportunity to revenge themselves upon a creature regarded by Indians as so mighty, it must not be of this world.

3

The Earliest
Grizzly Attacks

As the frontier pushed westward, explorers and mountain men were destined to clash with the fearsome grizzly. Morphologically speaking, these grizzly bears were almost identical to those that today inhabit parts of the West and Northwest. But in attitude and temperament—at least judging from early accounts—they were something else indeed. The grizzly of yesteryear had little to fear from primitive Native Americans, brave as they might have been. The animal's slashing teeth and claws, lightning swiftness, and incredible ferocity were powerful weapons against the crude spears of the Indians. But this all changed when the white man's silhouette first appeared upon the horizon.

The first person of European descent to report on the grizzly might well have been Pedro de Castaneda, a member of Coronado's expedition. From 1540 to 1542, Coronado led his men through black and grizzly bear country, across wide plains and through the willow-choked river bottoms of territory now known as Colorado, Nebraska, Kansas, and New Mexico. When Castaneda wrote of "many bears," some of them had to be grizzlies.

Far to the west, Father Antonio de la Ascension took up the account. Father Antonio was the official recorder for Sebastian Vizcaino, a merchant mariner commissioned by Mexico City's viceroy to locate a port on the coast of California. Such a port would provide a safe haven for the crown's vessels and would provide needed protection for Spanish shipping interests.

On 16 December 1602, Vizcaino sailed into a bay he named Monterey. Father Antonio became possibly the first white man to describe the California grizzly after he watched the great beasts feed one evening on a dead whale that had washed up on the beach. The priest noted with some awe that the tracks of these bears measured "a good third of a yard long and a hand wide."

Henry Kelsey, an explorer of the old Hudson's Bay Company, was the first to write of plains grizzlies while his party traversed the Canadian prairies. The date in Kelsey's journal was 19 August 1691, almost a century after Father Antonio's entries:

> . . . This plan affords Nothin but short Round sticky grass & Buffillo & a great Bear which is Bigger than any white Bear & is neither White nor Black But silver hair'd like our English Rabbitt . . .

Kelsey, together with his Indian guide, later ran smack dab into two grizzlies. The bears were as surprised as the men. They bluff-charged and then bounded after the Indian, who, knowing the nature of grizzlies, climbed high into the top of a tree. Kelsey scrambled to the top of his own tree. The Englishman took aim, fired his flintlock musket, and killed one of the belligerent beasts. But when the first bear dropped, the second one turned to see the telltale puff of smoke from Kelsey's barrel. The bear came roaring up below Kelsey but was unable to detect the man clinging tightly to the branches of the swaying willow tree. Reluctantly the bear gave up on Kelsey and returned to the Indian, who was still crouching in terror on a limb. With the bear's attention diverted, Kelsey was able to reload, fire again, and kill the second bear. Kelsey's account is important because it may be the first documented report of an actual grizzly attack.

Later, Kelsey mentioned a bear that provided good meat for eating but whose hide he was discouraged from keeping because his Indian hosts "said it was God." Here are his exact words:

> And then you have beast of severall kind
> The one is a black Buffillo great
> Another is an outgrown Bear wch. is good meat
> His skin to gett I have used all ye ways I can
> He is mans food & he makes food of man
> His hide they would not me it preserve
> But said it was god & they should Starve
> This plain affords nothing but Beast & grass . . .

Although the great grizzled bear was not yet known by the name that would make him the most feared beast upon the continent, Alfred Barnaby Thomas, in writing the 1719 *Diary of the Campaign of Governor Antonio de Valverde against the Ute and Comanche Indians*, gave us this account of life at the time in what is now New Mexico and Colorado:

> . . . On this day a mountain lion and a wildcat were killed. At about sunset some Indians came in running from a bear, which plunged into the middle of the camp, throwing the people into confusion. With great shouting and uproar, they killed him with many spear thrusts and arrows. His strength and size were so formidable that the governor was impelled to go with the chaplain to view it.

What else but a grizzly could have prompted Thomas to make such an entry? To provide a small idea of the great bears' abundance at the time, the entry of 6 October 1719, logged in just a few days afterward, reaffirms the expedition's continuing problems with these magnificent predators:

> . . . On this day before the halt [to erect a camp] a bear was met. It was larger than the preceding ones for its size and height [probably estimated to the withers or back] were probably greater than that of a donkey. One of the soldiers went out and put a spear into him up to the middle of the shaft. The brute turning around seized the lance, and grasped the horse by the hocks. At the same time another soldier went to the rescue and gave the bear another spear thrust. The bear, seizing the horse by the tail, held him down and clawing viciously, tore a piece of flesh off the rump. Having tied the bear up finally, they finished killing him. The soldiers who were bringing up the rear guard of the cavalry met a female and two cubs, which they also killed.

John Long, in relating his travels during 1768 and 1788, also mentioned the grizzly. He explained in detail how local Indians almost always tried to kill this animal. "The instant [the Indians] see one, they endeavour to surround it, by forming a large circle. If it is on the march they fire at it."

In the book *California Grizzly*, authors Traci Storer and Lloyd Tevis tell how in 1776 Fray Pedro Font accompanied the Anza expedition to what is now Crystal Springs Lake south of San Francisco. Font wrote in his diary of the many grizzlies that were abroad, and that "they often attack and do damage to the Indians when they go to hunt, of which I saw many horrible examples." In 1772, grizzlies around Mission San Luis Obispo were extremely destructive. Records reveal that "not a few of the Indians showed that they had been lacerated and maimed by [the bears'] terrible claws." In 1792, Jose Longinos Martines wrote that bears killed many Indians: ". . . within a short time I have seen two dead gentiles, victims of this ferocious animal."

The early Spanish who settled California soon learned that to ingratiate themselves with local Indians all they had to do was destroy every grizzly they encountered. And destroy them they did, to the delight of the Indians, who showered their saviors with gifts. The writings of Fray Franciso Palou, recounted in *California Grizzly,* include the following observations:

> Although in that region there was no village of any kind, the Indians soon began to arrive . . . it had been only three months since the soldiers had been there at the time of the slaughter of the bears (for which they were very thankful, as the land had been rid of these fierce animals, who had killed many of the Indians, of whom not a few of those who were still alive showed the terrible scars of their dreadful claws), they were glad to show themselves delighted that our people had come among them to live. They began to visit the Mission with great frequency, bringing little presents of venison and wild grains to the Father.

California grizzlies, which had run roughshod up and down the coast for thousands of years, seemed to grow quite contemptuous of the Spaniards, who were now flooding the countryside. If a pueblo lay in a grizzly's path, the bear would often amble through, sometimes with other bears—most likely cubs—scattering townspeople in every direction. Although these unwanted visitors usually minded their own business, occasionally one would fly into a rage.

When James O. Pattie visited Monterey in the 1820s, he wrote that "numberless grey bears are frequently known to attack men."

The situation was similar in the Canadian northwest, where in 1793, Sir Alexander MacKenzie took note of the grizzly. "We saw this day two grisly and hideous bears." The origin of the name grizzly could be a derivative of "grisly," a name used by early explorers like MacKenzie to identify what, to them, were *grisly* killers of men. Or it may have come from the word "grizzled," which was used to describe the great bears' distinctive, silver-tipped pelage.

But this much is certain: Grizzlies had been kings of their domain for nearly as long as they'd inhabited the continent. They were plentiful and they were bold, roaming most of the West—both plains and mountains— with impunity. And they seemed little inclined to share their kingdom with anyone else.

4

Lewis and Clark and the Grizzly

When white men first encountered the grizzly, the bear rarely backed down, as you will see in these accounts from the journals of Meriwether Lewis and William Clark during their two-year journey (1804-1805) in search of the Northwest Passage.

The first mention of great numbers of grizzly bears, or white bears, as Lewis and Clark called them, occurred on 1 October 1804 with a report by Clark from what is now the state of South Dakota just north of the mouth of the Cheyenne ("Chien" to Clark) River. Sadly, wildlife officials in South Dakota today report that bears of any kind are rarely seen there.

1 October 1804

. . . The Black Mountains (Black Hills), he (Mr. Jean Valle) says, are very high, and some parts retain snow even in the summer. (There) are no beaver on Cheyenne River, but there are great numbers of goats on the mountains and a kind of animal nearly the size of an elk only with large, circular horns (Rocky Mountain sheep). White bears (grizzlies) are also plentiful.

After wintering in the Mandan Indian villages of North Dakota, Captain Lewis seemed eager to encounter the ferocious white bear of which he had heard so much:

13 April 1805

. . . We also saw many enormous tracks of the white bear along the river shore and among the carcasses of the buffalo, upon which I presume they feed. We have not yet seen one of these animals, though their tracks are abundant and recent. The men, as well as ourselves, are anxious to meet with some of these bears. The Indians, who never dare to attack this animal unless they are in parties of from six to ten people, give a formidable account of the strength and ferocity of the white bear. Even then, they are frequently defeated, often losing one or more of their party. The Indians attack these bears with bows and arrows and the indifferent guns furnished to them by the traders which they shoot so uncertainly and at so short a distance that they frequently miss and fall sacrifice to the bear. (Unless a bear is shot through the head or heart, the wound is usually not mortal).

Upon meeting a man, the white bear is said to more frequently attack than to flee. Before the Indians go in quest of the white bear, they paint themselves and perform all those superstitious rites commonly observed when they are about to make war on a neighboring tribe . . .

Lewis and Clark soon had more bear excitement than they could handle. Bear encounters of the closest kind occurred at a rapid rate, but their very first one did little to substantiate the grizzly's reputation for fierceness. Lewis, at least, seemed almost disdainful as he wrote about the ease with which the first white bear (which was actually a light brown or yellow) was dispatched:

29 April 1805
(in what is now far eastern Montana)

Set out this morning at the usual hour. The wind was moderate. I walked on shore with one man. At about 8:00 A.M. we fell in with two brown or yellow bear, both of which we wounded. One made his escape; after firing on the other it pursued me 70 or 80 yards but had been so badly wounded he was unable to get so close as to keep me from recharging my gun. We repeated our fire and killed him. It was a male, not yet fully grown, and we estimated his weight at about 300 pounds, although there was no way we could be certain of this. The legs of this bear are somewhat longer than those of the black as are its talons and tusks incomparably larger and longer. The testicles, which in the black bear are placed well back between the thighs and contained in one pouch like those of the dog and most quadrupeds, are suspended in separated pouches. (Lewis erred in describing the grizzly's scrotum, which is contained in but a single sac.) Its color is yellowish-brown; the eyes small, black, and piercing. The front of the forelegs near the feet is usually black and the fur is finer, thicker, and deeper than that of the black bear. It is a much more furious and formidable animal and will frequently pursue the hunter when wounded. It is astonishing to see the wounds they will bear before they can be killed. The Indians may well fear this animal equipped as they generally are with their bows and arrows or indifferent fusees, but in the hands of skillful riflemen they are by no means as formidable or dangerous as they have been represented.

5 May 1805 (Captain Lewis)

This evening Captain Clark and Drouilliard killed the largest brown bear we have yet seen. It was a tremendous-looking animal and extremely hard to kill.

Notwithstanding he had five balls through his lungs and five others in various parts, he was still able to swim more than half the distance across the river to a sand bar, and it was at least another twenty minutes before he died. He did not attempt to attack, but fled, and made the most tremendous roaring from the moment he was shot. We had no means of weighing this monster. Captain Clark thought he would weigh 500 pounds. For my own part, I think the estimate too small by 100 pounds. He measured eight feet 7 inches from the nose to the extremity of the hind feet; five feet 10 inches around the breast; one foot eleven inches around the middle of the arm; and three feet eleven inches around the neck. His talons, which numbered five on each foot, measured $4^3/_8$ inches in length. . . .

From this date on, bear confrontations began to escalate. The very next day, a grizzly swam the Missouri just upstream of the advancing party. On 11 May, Bratton, one of the party, shot a bear that immediately turned on him and pursued him a great distance. Captain Lewis, together with seven of his men, joined Bratton to finish off the "monster." When they found him skulking back in some thick brush, they shot him through the skull twice. Lewis then confesses, with classic understatement:

We now found that Bratton had shot him through the center of the lungs, notwithstanding which, the bear had still pursued him (Bratton) near half a mile and then had returned (to the thick brush) more than double that distance and with his talons had prepared himself a bed in the earth about two feet deep and five feet long and was perfectly alive when we found him, which could not have been less than two hours after he had received the wound.

These bears, being so hard to die, rather intimidate us all. I must confess that I do not like the gentlemen and had rather fight two Indians than one bear. There is no other chance to conquer them by a single shot but by shooting them through the brains, and this becomes difficult in consequence of two large muscles, which cover the sides of the forehead, and the sharp projection of the center of the frontal bone, which is also of a pretty good thickness. The fleece and skin were as much as two men could carry.

One of the most thrilling bear attacks of the entire expedition took place on 14 May 1805. As with most of the party's encounters, this attack was provoked by the men.

In the evening the men in two of the rear canoes discovered a large brown bear lying in the open about 300 paces from the river, and six of them went out to attack him. They were all good hunters and took the advantage of a small eminence which concealed them and got to within 40 paces of him without being seen. Two of them reserved their fire; the four others fired nearly at the same time and each put his bullet through him. Two of the balls passed through the bulk of both lobes of his lungs. In an instant, this monster ran at them with open mouth. The two who had not yet fired discharged their pieces as he came toward them. Both struck him, one only slightly, and the other fortunately broke his shoulder. This, however, only retarded his motion for a moment. The men, unable to reload their guns, took to flight. The bear pursued and had very nearly overtaken them before they reached the river; two of the party betook themselves to a canoe. The others separated and concealed themselves among the willows, reloaded, and each discharged his piece as he had an opportunity. They struck him several more times but the guns only served to direct the bear to them. In this manner he pursued two of them separately so closely that they were obliged to throw aside their guns and pouches and throw themselves into the river although the bank was nearly 20 feet high. So enraged was this animal that he plunged into the river only a few feet behind the second man who had taken refuge in the water, when one of the men who still remained on shore shot the bear through the head and finally killed him. They then took him out on shore and butchered him and found eight balls had passed through him in different directions. . . .

The expedition ran into the great bears everywhere. On 19 May 1805 Lewis wrote, "Captain Clark walked on shore with two of the hunters and killed a brown bear . . . it was shot through the heart [but] ran at its usual pace nearly a quarter of a mile before it fell . . ."

One of the final entries about grizzly bears was made on 15 July 1806. Lewis, who by now was clearly awe-struck by the animals, wrote the following after waiting for Drouilliard to return from a scouting expedition:

His (Drouilliard's) safe return has relieved me from great anxiety. I had already settled it in my mind that a white bear had killed him, and should have set out tomorrow in search of him, and if I could not find him to continue my route to Maria's River. I knew that if he met with a bear, in the plains even, he would attack him; and that, if any accident should happen to sepa-rate him from his horse in that situation, the chances in favor of his being killed would be as 9 to 10. I felt so perfectly satisfied that he had returned in safety, that I thought but little of the horses [that had been stolen by Indians], although they were seven of the best I had.

5

Tales of Hugh Glass and Jedediah Smith

The Saga of Hugh Glass

A couple of the most famous—and most oft-documented—grizzly bear attacks on record are those that befell two of Major Andrew Henry's party. Major Henry had been chosen to help lead General William H. Ashley's "enterprising young men" into the pristine fur-trapping country of the Northwest. It promised to be a rugged journey, one guaranteed to test the mettle of even the most stalwart frontiersman, since it retraced a good percentage of both the steps and the oar-strokes of Lewis and Clark.

The party survived a number of harrowing Indian engagements, most notably with the treacherous Arikaras, or "Rees." In September 1823, in the far northwestern corner of what is now South Dakota, Henry led a party of men overland in a shortcut up the Grand River Valley that took them well away from the Missouri River. His objective: the country of the Yellowstone, where he planned to establish a winter camp.

One of Henry's men, Hugh Glass, was an independent fellow and had a different idea. Trapper and journalist Jim Clyman attested to this, saying ". . . a Mr. Hugh Glass . . . who would not be restrained . . . went off the line of march one afternoon and met with a large grizzly bear, which he shot and wounded. The bear, as is usual, attacked Glass." Stanley Vestal, in his biography *Jim Bridger, Mountain Man*, describes it like this:

> On the fifth day, old Hugh Glass and a companion were hunting in advance of the party. Glass was in the lead . . . forcing his way through a dense thicket of plum bushes. The wild plums grow in sandy places, in thick clumps. When Glass came out of the thicket into a small clearing by the water, he found himself within a few paces of a huge she-bear and two sizable cubs lying on the warm sand.
>
> Glass knew he was in a terrible predicament. Hemmed in by the dense brush of the plum thicket, as Clyman reports, "He attempted to climb a tree but the bear caught him and hauled him to the ground, tearing and lacerating his body at a fearful rate." Other reports have the bear seizing Glass by the throat and lifting him well off the ground.
>
> Several of Glass's party heard the ruckus and ran to help the trapper. But they could not shoot for fear of hitting Glass. Finally, the bear finished. It reluctantly turned to leave, giving the men the opportunity for which they'd been waiting. Several men fired and a number of bullets hit home. But their considerable impact enraged the bear further. Once again it pounced on Glass, tearing and ripping anew his already severely wounded body. At last, however, their volleys did the job. The bear tumbled to the ground, mortally wounded.

In "The Chronicles of George C. Yount," the author, who was with Glass during the winter of 1828-29, recalled what Glass had told him of the attack:

The monster had seized him, torn the flesh from the lower part of the body, and from the lower limbs. He also had his neck shockingly torn, even to the degree that an aperture appeared to have been made into the windpipe, and his breath to exude at the side of his neck. It is not probable, however, that any aperture was made into the windpipe. Blood flowed freely, but fortunately no bone was broken, and his hands and arms were not disabled.

Glass had stumbled onto that most worrisome of all bear situations, a female grizzly with cubs. There's little doubt why the sow attacked, especially since a plum thicket wouldn't allow much room for either trapper or bear to maneuver. The big sow undoubtedly saw Glass as a threat to her youngsters and swiftly answered the threat in the only way she knew how: by attacking. And while a few people believe this tale to be untrue, others—among them most modern historians—believe that this famous attack actually took place.

If some doubt the truth of this attack, what transpired afterward is even more unbelievable. Major Henry convinced two of his party to stay with the mortally wounded Glass until he died. These two men remained with Glass for five days, taking care of the feverish man to the best of their limited abilities. As the days dragged on, though, they became frightened for themselves. The land was crawling with both four-legged and two-legged predators, and the two men eventually decided to leave Glass to the elements. They believed nothing they could do would save him. They made him as comfortable as possible, then took Glass's rifle and ammunition and set out to rejoin their party. Leaving Glass was bad enough, but taking his muzzleloader and ammunition was unforgivable, a violation of the code of the frontiersman. Had the Rees discovered Glass's presence, confronting the she-bear would have probably been preferable. By leaving Glass unarmed, the two men signed the trapper's death sentence.

The talk of the time was that the two shady fellows chosen to guard Glass were named Fitzgerald and Bridger. In later years, however, Jim Bridger's character was judged so impeccable under so many diverse and adverse conditions that most people find it difficult to believe that he would have abandoned Glass under any circumstances, so long as the man drew breath.

In 1839 Edmund Flagg reported that Glass had been left with two men named Fitzgerald and Bridges. There was indeed a trapper named Bridges who worked the Missouri that year. Alpheus H. Favour in his book *Old Bill Williams* reveals that James Bridges was a contemporary frontiersman on the Missouri. It is but a short jump from a man named James Bridges to the more famous—and infinitely more interesting—James Bridger.

In any event, Glass was abandoned. By whom, we will probably never know for sure. But the tough old codger did not die. Fevered and suffering from a terrible thirst, he managed to rouse himself enough to crawl to a nearby spring, "where he lay for ten days." During this time, he ate ripe chokecherries and buffalo berries. Once Glass had regained some strength, the mountain man took his bearings and set off for Fort Kiowa, 350 miles away, armed with just the straight-edge razor he'd been carrying inside his wallet. Along the way, he encountered a pack of wolves that had just killed a buffalo calf. He dragged himself among them, daring the hungry critters to take the bloody carcass. With the aid of a flint, his razor, and a pile of dry leaves, he managed to light a fire. When the wolves slunk away, Glass tore into the meat, too famished to wait the time it would take to cook it. In a test of endurance made all the more remarkable because of the severity of his wounds, Glass crawled and walked to Fort Kiowa.

If we are to believe the legends, Glass experienced many more adventures before confronting his old traitorous acquaintance, possibly the man Fitzgerald. When finally he did, Glass obtained the rifle that had been stolen from him, along with the other gear he would need to return fully equipped to the field. One can only imagine the look on this scoundrel's face as he gazed at the man he thought had died on the prairie.

The bear attack made Glass a celebrity. He gave many talks and interviews about his incredible feat. Slyly, the man never divulged the names of the two caretakers who had so carelessly left him to die. The possibility that Glass concocted much of this tale is strong because not only would he never name names, but also neither of these so-called caretakers ever came forward with their own versions of the tale. And during a time when such stories were eagerly awaited, from rogue and hero alike, that in itself is extremely odd.

❖   ❖   ❖

Jedediah Smith and the Badland Grizzly

A few weeks before Hugh Glass's fateful encounter with the grizzly sow and her cubs, Jedediah Smith led a small party of men westward from the same Fort Kiowa. The first night, Jedediah dropped down into the valley of what James Clyman called "White Clay Creek, a tributary running thick with a strange white sediment and resembling cream in appearance but of a sweetish, pungent taste."

Smith and his legion continued west until they struck the South Fork of the Cheyenne River a few miles below the place where it emerged from the Black Hills. They crossed the river and entered the badlands. Jedediah hoped that the company would find enough beaver so that the party might rest for a while. As the group moved through a brushy bottom, a large grizzly came charging down the valley. He barged right through the line of horses and men, then turned and ran parallel with them. Jedediah, who had been at the front of the entourage, galloped toward open ground, but as he emerged from the thicket, he ran headlong into the bear.

Jim Clyman picks up the story:

> . . . Grizzly did not hesitate even a moment but sprang on the captain, taking him by the head first, pitching him sprawling upon the earth. He grabbed him by the middle but fortunately caught [the captain] by the ball pouch and butcher knife, which he broke. [The bear] broke several of the captain's ribs and cut his head badly.
>
> None of us had any surgical knowledge or knew what should be done. One said, "come take hold," and he would say "why not you," and so it went around. I asked the Captain what was best and he said, "One or two of [you should go] for water, and if you have a needle and thread get it out and sew up the wounds around my head," which was bleeding freely. I got a pair of scissors and cut off his hair and then began my first job of dressing his wounds. Upon examination, I found the bear had taken nearly all his head in his capacious mouth from his left eye on one side close to his right ear on the other, laying the skull bare to near the crown of the head, leaving a white streak where his teeth [had] passed. One of his ears was torn from his head out to the outer rim. After stitching all his other wounds in the best way I was capable and according to the Captain's directions—the ear being the last—I told him I could do nothing for his ear. "Oh, you must try to stitch it up some way or the other," said he. Then I put in my needle, stitching it through and through and over and over, laying the lacerated parts together as nice as I could with my hands. Water was found in about a mile when we all moved down and encamped, the Captain being able to mount his horse and ride to camp where we pitched a tent, the only one we had, and made him as comfortable as circumstances would

permit. This gave us a lesson on the character of the grizzly bear which we did not forget.

The Smith family insists to this day that Jedediah killed his bear. Mountain tradition, however, held that Arthur Black, Jedediah's later companion on the Pacific slope, once saved him from a bear attack. Although it's uncertain whether Arthur Black accompanied Jedediah Smith on this, his first journey west, this may indeed have been the time Black saved Smith's life.

Jedediah Smith bore the marks of this attack until the end of his all-too-brief life. His eyebrow had been completely ripped off, and his ear was tattered and had healed in a half-cocked position on his head. To mitigate the stares of the curious, Jedediah allowed his hair to grow long so that it hung down well below what was left of his ears.

6

Tales of the Mountain Men

As early-nineteenth-century trappers, hunters, and explorers ventured into the strongholds of the grizzly bear, confrontations increased at an exponential rate. Bears weren't used to backing down from humans, which they'd once almost certainly regarded as puny. And the very notion of backing down in any way was completely foreign to a mountain man. Grizzly bears began to acquire a reputation; many of the frontier's most notable personalities reported incidents with these animals. And in the lexicon of the day, "incidents" meant attacks. Trouble for the continent's big bears began to brew as one after another of the mountain men wrote or related his harrowing tale of terror.

❖   ❖   ❖

Ezekiel Williams on the Arkansas River

It was the year 1807. Trapper Ezekiel Williams recruited twenty men and led them up the Missouri River. The little party reached the mouth of the Yellowstone and began trapping its Rocky Mountain feeder streams. According to David H. Coyners, Williams's biographer, relentless Indian attacks eventually separated the men. Williams found himself alone. He worked his way southward to the Arkansas River and then followed it downstream, trapping as he went, eventually accumulating an enviable load of beaver pelts, or plews. Williams reached the Missouri two years later. Along the way it was all but inevitable that he would experience trouble with grizzlies.

Some authorities dispute Coyners's account. Others find it difficult to disbelieve since so many minute details are provided. The tale is so interesting, however, that any compilation of noteworthy North American bear attacks would be incomplete without it:

> . . . His [Captain Williams's] usual plan was to glide along down the stream, until he came to a place where beaver signs were abundant. There he would push his little bark to the shore, into some eddy among the willows, where he remained concealed, except when he was setting his traps or visiting them in the morning. He always set his traps between sunset and dark, and visited them at the earliest break of day. When he had taken all of the beaver in one neighborhood, he would untie his little conveyance and glide onward and downward to try his luck in another place.
>
> . . . The upper part of the Arkansas (for this proved to be the river upon which he was trapping) is very destitute of timber, and the prairie frequently begins at the bank of the river and expands on either side as far as the eye can see. . . Williams never used his rifle to procure meat, except when it was absolutely necessary and when it could be done with perfect safety. On one occasion, when he had no beaver flesh, upon which he generally subsisted, he killed a deer, and after refreshing an empty stomach with a portion of it, he placed the carcass, which he had cut up, in one end of his canoe. As it was his invariable custom to sleep in his canoe, the night after he had laid in a supply

45

of venison he was startled in his sleep by the trampling of something in the bushes on the bank. Tramp, tramp, tramp went the footstep, as it approached the canoe. Captain Williams first thought it might be an Indian that had found out his locality, but an Indian would not approach him in that careless manner. Although there was a beautiful starlight, yet the shade of the trees and a dense undergrowth made it very dark on the bank of the river. Captain Williams always adopted the precaution of tying his canoe to shore with a piece of rawhide about twenty feet long, which let it swing from the bank about that distance. This precaution he adopted at night, so that in an emergency he might cut the cord that bound him to the shore, and glide off without any noise. During the day he hid his canoe in the willows.

As the sound of the footsteps grew more and more distinct, the captain observed a huge grizzly bear approach the edge of the water and hold up its head as if scenting something. He then let his huge body into the water and made for the canoe. Captain Williams snatched up his ax as the most suitable means of defending himself in such a scrape, and stood with it uplifted and ready to drive it into the head of the huge aggressor. The bear reached the canoe, and immediately placed his forepaws upon the hind end of it, and nearly turned it over. Captain Williams struck one of his feet with the edge of his ax, which caused him to relax his hold with that foot. He, however, held on with the other foot, and Captain Williams inflicted another blow upon his head, which caused him to let the canoe go entirely. Captain Williams thought the bear had sunk in the water, from the stunning effects of the blow, and was drowned. He saw nothing more of him, nor did he hear anything. The presumption was, he went under the water. His aim had been to get at the fresh meat in the captain's canoe. The next morning, two of the bear's claws, severed from one of his feet by Captain

Williams's ax, lay in the canoe. They were carefully preserved by the resolute captain for a number of years as a trophy that he was fond of exhibiting and the history of which he delighted to detail.

❖ ❖ ❖

Zebulon Montgomery Pike

Zebulon Montgomery Pike, for whom central Colorado's Pike's Peak was named, was no stranger to grizzlies either. In a letter to Thomas Jefferson dated 3 February 1808, Pike wrote about circumstances surrounding the capture of two grizzly cubs that he had recently sent on to the president. It was obvious that Pike held grizzlies in high regard for two reasons: He felt they were reluctant to attack humans; and he was greatly impressed with the degree of their ferocity when ultimately confronted. This stood in stark contrast to the opinions expressed by his contemporaries, most of whom would go out of their way to kill one, no matter what.

> . . . Whilst in the mountains we sometimes discovered them [grizzlies] at a distance, but in no instance was ever able to come up with one, which we eagerly sought, and that being the most inclement season of the Year, induces me to believe they seldom or ever attack a man unprovoked, but defend themselves courageously—an instance of which occurred in New Mexico (whilst I sojourned in that province)—when three of the natives attack'd one with their lances two of whom he [the bear] killed, and wounded the third, before he [the bear] fell the Victim.

❖ ❖ ❖

William Cannon

Washington Irving, the famous early American writer, both gathered and edited accounts of various members of the Astoria Company. This incident took place in 1811 along the west-central part of what is now the border separating North and South Dakota:

> The hunters, both white and red men, consider [the grizzly bear] the most heroic game. They prefer to hunt him on horseback and will venture so near as sometimes to singe his hair with the flash of the rifle. The hunter of the grizzly bear, however, must be an experienced hand and know where to aim at a vital part; for of all quadrupeds he is the most difficult to kill. He will receive repeated wounds without flinching, and rarely is a shot mortal unless through the head or heart.

That the dangers posed by the grizzly bear at this night encampment were not imaginary was proved on the following morning. Among the hired men of the party was one William Cannon, who had been a soldier at one of the frontier posts and had entered into the employ of Mr. Hunt at Mackinaw. He was an inexperienced hunter and a poor shot, for which he was much bantered by his more adroit comrades. Piqued at their raillery, he had been practicing ever since he had joined the expedition, but without success. In the course of the present afternoon, he went forth by himself to take a lesson in venery and, to his great delight, had the good fortune to kill a buffalo. As he was a considerable distance from the camp, he cut out the tongue and some of the choice bits, made them into a parcel, and, slinging them on his shoulders by a strap passed around his forehead, as the *voyageurs* carry packages of goods, set out all glorious for the camp, anticipating a triumph over his brother hunters.

In passing through a narrow ravine, he heard a noise behind him, and, looking around, beheld, to his dismay a grizzly bear in full pursuit, apparently attracted by the scent of the meat. Cannon had heard so much of the invulnerability of this tremendous animal that he never attempted to fire. Slipping the strap from his forehead, he let go the buffalo meat and ran for his life. The bear did not stop to regale himself with the meat but kept on after the hunter. He had nearly overtaken him when Cannon reached a tree and, throwing down his rifle, scrambled up it. The next instant the bruin was at the foot of the tree; but, as this species of bear does not climb, he contented himself with turning the chase into a blockade. Night came on. In the darkness Cannon could not perceive whether or not the enemy maintained his station; but his fears pictured him rigorously mounting guard. He passed the night, therefore, in the tree, a prey to dismal fancies. In the morning the bear was gone. Cannon warily descended the tree, gathered up his gun, and made the best of his way back to the camp without venturing to look after his buffalo meat.

❖   ❖   ❖

John Day

Irving recounted yet another grizzly bear adventure, which, for a change, was somewhat humorous. Kentuckian John Day figured prominently in this tale, which took place slightly farther along the trail than the preceding one:

> . . . Day was hunting in company with one of the clerks of the company, a lively youngster, who was a great favorite with the veteran but whose vivacity he had continually to keep in check. They were in search of deer when suddenly a huge grizzly bear emerged from a thicket about thirty yards distant, rearing himself upon his hind legs with a terrific growl and displaying a hideous array of teeth and claws. The rifle of the young man was leveled in an instant, but John Day's iron hand was as quickly upon his arm. "Be quiet, boy! Be quiet!" exclaimed the hunter between his clenched teeth, and without turning his eyes from the bear. They remained motionless. The monster regarded them for a

time, then, lowering himself on his forepaws, slowly withdrew. He had not gone many paces before he again returned, reared himself on his hind legs, and repeated the menace. Day's hand was still on the arm of his young companion; he again pressed it hard and kept repeating between his teeth, "Quiet, boy! Keep quiet!— Keep quiet!" though the latter had not made a move since his first prohibition. The bear again lowered himself on all fours, retreated some twenty yards far- ther, and again returned, reared, showed his teeth and growled. This third menace was too much for the game spirit of John Day. "By Jove!" exclaimed he, "I can stand this no longer," and in an instant a ball from his rifle whizzed into the foe. The wound was not mortal; but, luckily, it dismayed instead of enraged the animal, and he retreated into the thicket.

Day's young companion reproached him for not practicing the caution which he enjoined upon others. "Why, boy," replied the veteran, "caution is caution, but one must not put up with too much, even from a bear. Would you have me suffer myself to be bullied all day by a varmint?"

❖ ❖ ❖

Lewis Dawson

By 1821 the face of the West was changing daily as marchers of every description advanced across its plains and plunged into its virgin stands of timber. Students of history remain indebted to those men who, like Jacob Fowler, were inspired to keep journals. Fowler's description of a grizzly bear attack on Lewis Dawson contains the first record of any white American citizen dying and being buried within the area now known as Colorado.

Tuesday, 13 November 1821. . . . We stopped here about one o'clock and sent back for one horse that was not able to keep up. We found some grapes among the brush. While some [of us] were hunting and others cooking and some picking grapes, a gun was fired and the cry of a white bear raised. We were all armed in an instant and each man ran his own course to look for the desperate animal. The brush in which we camped contained from ten to twenty acres into which the bear had run for shelter, finding himself surrounded on all sides. Through this [brush] Colonel Glanns [together] with four other [men] attempted to run. But the bear, being in their way, lay close in the brush, undiscovered till they were within a few feet of it when it sprang up and caught Lewis Dawson and pulled him down. In an instant, Colonel Glanns' gun misfired or he would have relieved the man. But a large slut [a dog] which belongs to the party attacked the bear with such fury that it [the bear] left the man and pursued [the dog] a few steps in which time the man got up and ran a few steps but was [again] overtaken by the bear. When the Colonel made a second attempt to shoot, his gun misfired again and the slut, as before, relieved the man who ran as before but who was soon again in the grasp of the bear [which] seemed intent on his destruction. Colonel Glanns again ran close up and as before his gun would not go off. The slut now made another attack and relieved the man. The Colonel now became alarmed lest the bear would pursue him also and ran up a stoop[ed over] tree, and after him, the wounded man, who was followed by the bear. And thus they were all three up one tree. But [another] tree [was] standing in reach, [so] the Colonel stepped over on that [one], and let the man and bear pass till the bear caught Dawson by one leg and drew him backwards down the tree. While this was going on, the Colonel sharpened his flint, primed his gun and shot the bear down while it was pulling the man by the leg [and] before any of the party arrived to relieve him. But the bear soon rose again and was shot by several other men who had got up to the place of action. It is to be remarked that the other three men with him ran off, and the brush was so thick that those outside were some time getting through [it].

51

I was myself down the creek, below the brush, and heard the dreadful screams of the man in the clutches of the bear, the yelping of the slut and the hollering of the men to "Run in, Run in. The man will be killed!" And knowing the distance [to be] so great that I [knew I] could not get there in time to save the man. So it is much easier to imagine my feelings than [to] describe them, but before I got to the place of action the bear was killed and I met the wounded man with Robert Fowler and one or two more assisting him [back] to camp where his wounds were examined. It appears his head was in the bear's mouth at least twice, and that when the monster gave the crush that mashed the man's head (it being too large for the span of his mouth) the head slipped out, [but] the teeth cut the skin to the bone wherever they touched it so that the skin of the head was cut from about the ears to the [crown] in several directions. All of [the] wounds were sewed up as well as could be done by men in our situation, [with] no surgeon nor surgical instruments. The man still retained his understanding but said, "I am killed; I heard my skull break." But we were willing to believe he was mistaken as he spoke cheerfully on the subject until the afternoon of the second day when he began to be restless and somewhat delirious. And on examining a hole in the upper part of his right temple, which we [had] believed [to be] only skin deep, we found the brains working [their way] out. We then supposed that he did hear his skull break. He lived till a little before day[light] on the third day after being wounded, all [of] which time we lay at camp, and [then] we buried him as well as our means would admit. Immediately after the fatal accident, and [after] having done all we could for the wounded man, we turned our attention to the bear and found him [to be] a large, fat animal. We skinned him, but found the smell of a polecat so strong, that we could not eat the meat. On examining his mouth we found that three of his teeth were broken off near the gums which we supposed was the cause of his not killing the man at the first bite. The one [tooth] not broke to be the cause of the hole in the right temple which killed the man at last. The hunter killed two deer and cased the skins for baggs, so we dried out the bear's oil and carried it with us. The skin was also taken care of.

On the West Coast, grizzlies continued to deal fits to the settlers. In January 1827, A. Duhaut-Cilly wrote that "bears are very common in the environs and without going farther than five or six leagues from San Francisco, they are often seen in herds." When describing numbers of grizzlies in the Napa Valley, George C. Yount emphasized that "they were every where—upon the plains, in the valleys, and on the mountains. . .so that I have often killed as many as five or six in one day, and it was not unusual to see fifty or sixty within the twenty-four hours."

❖   ❖   ❖

Jedediah Smith: Attacked Again!

On 8 March 1828, one of mountain man Jedediah Smith's companions, Harrison Rogers, killed one grizzly bear and wounded another in the Sacramento Valley. What follows happened, according to Smith's journal, the next morning:

> Mr. Rogers went after the wounded bear in company with John Hanna. In a short time Hanna came running in and said they had found the bear in a very bad thicket. That he [the bear] suddenly rose from his bed and rushed on them. Mr. Rogers fired a moment before the bear caught him. After biting him in several places he went off, but Hanna shot him again, when he [the bear] returned, [he] caught Mr. Rogers and gave him several additional wounds. I went out with a horse to bring him in and found him very badly wounded being severely cut in . . . 10 or 12 different places. I washed his wounds and dressed them with plasters of soap and sugar. (Mr. Rogers did not recover from his wounds for more than two weeks.)

On 31 March, Smith's party killed two grizzlies on the Sacramento River near the mouth of Chico Creek. The following day they brought down another bear, which had a stone arrowhead as well as a section of shaft inside its body. Smith described this adventure:

> In the evening we shot several bear and they ran into thickets . . . Several of us followed one that was badly wounded . . . We went on foot because the thicket was too close to admit a man on horseback.
>
> As we advanced I saw one and shot him in the head when he immediately . . . fell, apparently dead. I went in to bring him out without reloading my gun and when I arrived within four yards of the place where the bear lay, the man that was following me close behind spoke and said, "He is alive." I told him in answer that he was certainly dead and was observing the one I had shot so intently that I did not see the one that lay close by his side, which was the one to which the man behind me had reference to. At that moment the bear sprang toward us with open mouth and making no pleasant noise.
>
> Fortunately, the thicket was close on the bank of the creek and the second spring I plunged head foremost into the water. The bear ran over the man next to me and made a furious rush on the third man, Joseph Lapoint. But Lapoint had . . . a bayonet fixed on his gun and as the bear came in he gave him a severe wound in the neck, which induced him to change his course and run into another thicket close at hand. We followed him there and found another in company with him. One of them we killed and the other went off badly wounded.
>
> I then went on horseback with two men to look for another that was wounded. I rode up close to the thicket in which I supposed him to be and rode around it several times hallooing but without making any discovery. I rode up for a last look when the bear sprang for the horse. He was so close that the horse could not be got underway before he caught him by the tail. The horse being strong and much frightened . . . [exerted] himself so powerfully that he gave the bear no opportunity to

close upon him and actually drew him 40 or 50 yards before he [the bear] relinquished his hold.

The bear did not continue the pursuit but went off and [I] . . . returned to camp to feast on the spoils and talk of the incidents of our eventful hunt.

When reading the tales of Jedediah Smith, one can't help but get the distinct impression that if the man hadn't met his end as historians suppose he did—at the hands of hostile Comanches on the banks of the Cimarron River—he most certainly would have wound up "going under" due to a grizzly attack.

The year was 1831, the locale Colorado's arid southeastern mountains. Messalino, a man of Spanish descent who had been hired to guide Captain John Gunnison, already seemed to understand better than most men of his day the awesome power of a griz. Messalino explained that whenever he saw a bear, he'd take a shot at it, but "I try to hit in the right spot . . . if I miss it, I have to run."

❖   ❖   ❖

Osborne Russell

Osborne Russell also wrote of grizzlies in his journal. This is his first account of the great bears:

. . . On the twentieth of August we started again to hunt meat. We left the fort and traveled about six miles when we discovered a grizzly bear digging and eating roots in a piece of marshy ground near a large bunch of willows. The mulatto [Russell's companion] approached within 100 yards and shot him through the left shoulder. [T]he [bear] gave a hideous growl and sprang into the thicket. The mulatto then said, "Let him go; he is a dangerous varmint," but not being acquainted with the nature of these animals I determined on making another trial and persuaded the mulatto to assist me. We walked around the bunch of willows where the bear lay, keeping close together, with our rifles ready [and] cocked and presented toward the bushes near the place where he had entered, when we heard a sullen growl about ten feet from us, which was instantly followed by a spring of the bear toward us. His enormous jaws [were] extended [and his] eyes [were] flashing fire. Oh Heavens! Was ever anything so hideous? We could not retain sufficient presence of mind to shoot at him but took to our heels, separating as we ran, the bear taking after me. [But] finding that I could outrun him he left and turned to the other who wheeled about and discharged his rifle covering the bear with smoke and fire. [But] the ball, however, missing him, he turned and bound[ed] toward me. I could go no further without jumping into a huge quagmire, which hemmed me on three sides. I was obliged to turn about and face him [as] he came within about ten paces of me, then [he] suddenly stopped and raised his ponderous body erect, mouth wide open, gazing at me with a beastly laugh. At this moment I pulled [the] trigger and I knew not what else to do—and hardly knew I did this—but it accidentally happened that my rifle was pointed toward the bear when I pulled and the ball pierc[ed] his heart. He gave one bound from me, uttered a deathly howl and fell dead. But I trembled as if I had an ague fit for half an hour after. We butchered him, as he was very fat, packed the meat and skin on our horses and returned to the fort with the trophies of our bravery, but I secretly determined in my own mind never to molest another wounded grizzly bear in a marsh or thicket.

Russell also preserved an idea of just how numerous these great bears once were. Here he was writing about the country near what is now northwest Wyoming:

. . . This is a beautiful country [with] the large plains widely extending on either side of the [Yellowstone] river [and] intersected with streams and occasional low spurs of mountains while thousands of buffalo may be seen in almost every direction and deer, elk and grizzly bear are abundant. The latter are more numerous than in any other part of the mountains [o]wing to the vast quantities of cherries, plums, and other wild fruit which this section of country affords. In going to visit my traps a distance of three or four miles early in the morning I have frequently seen seven or eight [bears] standing about the clumps of cherry bushes on their hind legs gathering cherries with surprising dexterity, not even deigning to turn their grizzly heads to gaze at the passing trapper but merely casting a sidelong glance at him without altering their position.

❖   ❖   ❖

Marie's Tale

Another trapper, Thomas James, wrote down his memories in a book entitled *Three Years Among the Indians and Mexicans*. In this book he recalled Marie, a French-Canadian trapper, who had once tangled with a grizzly bear.

After setting his traps one morning, Marie ". . . strolled out into the prairie for game, and soon perceived a large white bear rolling on the ground in the shade of a tree." Marie did what most mountain men would have: He shot at the great bear. But he missed, and the bear ignored him. Marie, who should have been thanking God for his good fortune, at least to this point, reloaded and tried again.

This time, his ball found its mark. Sort of. The wounded bear looked for its antagonist. James wrote, "His majesty, instantly, with ears set back, flew toward his enemy like an arrow . . ." Although Marie scampered away as quickly as possible, he had nowhere to run except out onto a beaver dam. This he did, but seeing the bear follow close on his heels, the plucky French-Canadian dived into the shallow beaver pond. Unfortunately for Marie, the bear did the same. Marie came up for air, knowing the bear was right there with him. When he surfaced, the bear grabbed for him. Marie dived deep, holding his breath until once more a lack of air forced him to the top. This game of cat and mouse continued for several minutes, much to Marie's dismay. The grizzly didn't mind. He had plenty of time to wait out the pesky trapper. Finally, Marie's luck ran out. The man surfaced. . . right under the enraged beast's chin.

The bear clamped its teeth on the trapper's head, sinking its giant canines in their entire length. One tooth penetrated the bottom of Marie's right jaw. Another pierced his right eye. But the trapper's troubles had only just begun. The bear swam for shore, towing the prize it held firmly in its teeth.

By this time Marie's partner had come running. With nothing to lose—and Marie's life possibly to gain—the man took aim and fired. His ball flew true and the great bear sank to the ground, wounded fatally in its head. Luckily, the shot had missed Marie by scant inches. "I saw him [Marie] six days afterward," recalled Thomas James, "with a swelling on his head an inch thick, and his food and drink gushed through the opening under his jaw made by the teeth of his terrible enemy."

❖   ❖   ❖

Thomas "Broken Hand" Fitzpatrick

One of the most exciting confrontations involved trapper and fur trader Thomas "Broken Hand" Fitzpatrick. It was 1832, and Fitzpatrick had returned to St. Louis from Pierre's Hole in present-day Idaho, to gather more supplies for his men. After purchasing everything he needed—food, trade goods, implements, lead, and black powder—Fitzpatrick turned westward for the mountains. Since the first supply train to arrive at the rendezvous would reap the highest profit—and garner the finest skins in trade—Fitzpatrick decided it would be good business to race ahead to inform everyone that his wagons were on their way. And it was dur-ing this ride that Broken Hand Fitzpatrick had his most famous brush with death.

Most everyone else had already arrived at Pierre's Hole in anticipation of a long bout of trading, drinking, and whoring, not necessarily in that order. The num-ber of participants already waiting expectantly included Bill Sublette, older brother of Fitzpatrick's trading part-ner, Milt Sublette. When Bill's wagons pulled in loaded high with the casks of corn whiskey that mountain men like Tom Fitzpatrick had been craving for the past year, and Fitz didn't come running, Bill sensed something was wrong. What had happened to Fitz?

Almost everyone who knew Fitzpatrick suspected the worst: trouble with the pesky Blackfeet. But the truth was even more ominous.

When Fitzpatrick left his lumbering caravan of wagons, he quirted his reluctant pony along the mountain trail. As he barreled from their sight in a cloud of dust, Fitz glanced over his shoulder and waved at his men, knowing that if all went well, they'd rejoin in a week or so. Now, though, he had to ride. And ride he did, for four long days, making excellent time. Fitz figured he could spare a few daylight hours to let his horse graze. So he sat down to rest and eat a quick lunch of venison jerky.

Suddenly, a bear scrambled across the rocks and raced toward him in what Fitzpatrick later recalled as "double-quick time." Fitz, never one to back down, stood up just as the bear slammed on its brakes. The grizzly reared high on its hind legs and glared at the man who dared to face him in such a brazen manner. Minutes passed as the two foes stared each other down.

"After discovering that I was in no ways bashful," Fitzpatrick later said, "[the bear] bowed, turned, and ran, and I did the same, and made for my horse."

Big mistake. Fitzpatrick obviously understood grizzlies well enough to know that an attitude of direct
confrontation could occasionally force a bruin to back
down. He probably also realized that running could be
interpreted as an invitation to chase you down and kill
you. Nevertheless, Fitzpatrick ran, and the grizzly
wheeled around to give chase. Fitzpatrick was fleet of
foot, so fleet he actually believed he'd be able to spring
into his saddle and race his mount away from the bear.
What Fitz neglected to figure into this equation was the
reaction of his horse, which was not pleased to see a
giant grizzly bearing down on him at full speed. Fitz
grabbed for the saddle and began swinging up, but it
was too late. His horse reared and bolted as the rank
smell of bear swirled around him. The man fell flat on
his back on the rocky ground, directly in front of the
enraged bear.

Once again, Fitzpatrick leaped to his feet to confront the grizzly. And once again, the bear beat a hasty
retreat. But it made one final mistake: It stopped to
snuffle through Fitzpatrick's store of jerky. In fact, when
recollecting the incident, Fitz realized that it was the
smell of a free lunch that had probably attracted
the animal in the first place. While the bear ripped
through the mountain man's gear, Fitzpatrick was no
less busy. "I crept to my gun," he later said, "keeping a
rock between him and me, and having reached it, took
deliberate aim and killed him on the spot."

❖ ❖ ❖

Zenas Leonard and the Trappers

Zenas Leonard also told of an unfortunate and
apparently unprovoked grizzly attack in his book,
Adventures of a Mountain Man. The heroes of Leonard's
account were a couple of trappers who shared his fire

soon after their close encounter. Here is the exact account as related by Leonard:

> . . . They [the two trappers] had meandered the creek till they came to beaver dams, where they set their traps and turned their horses out to pasture; and were busily engaged in constructing a camp to pass the night in, when they discovered, at a short distance off, a tremendous large Grizzly Bear, rushing upon them at a furious rate.— They immediately sprang to their rifles which were standing at a tree hard-by, one of which was single triggered and the other double [set] triggered; unfortunately in the hurry, the one that was accustomed to the single trigger, caught up the double [set] triggered gun, and when the bear came upon him, not having set the trigger, he could not get his gun off; and the animal approaching within a few feet of him, he was obliged to commence beating it over the head with his gun. Bruin, thinking this rather rough usage, turned his attention to the man with the single triggered gun, who, in trying to set the trigger (supposing he had the double triggered gun) had fired it off, and was also obliged to beating the ferocious animal with his gun; finally, it left them without doing much injury, except tearing the sleeve off one of their coats and biting him through the hand. Four men were immediately dispatched for the traps, who returned in the evening with seven or eight beaver. The Grizzly Bear is the most ferocious animal that inhabits these prairies, and they are very numerous. They no sooner see you than they will make at you with open mouth. If you stand still, they will come within two or three yards of you, and stand upon their hind feet, and look you in the face, if you have fortitude enough to face them, they will turn and run off; but if you turn they will most certainly tear you to pieces; furnishing strong proof of the fact, that no wild beast, however daring and ferocious, unless wounded, will attack the face of a man.

Although Zenas Leonard was astute enough to realize that a brave man could sometimes stand up to an aggressive bear, even in extremely close quarters, his assumption that "no wild beast, . . . unless wounded, will attack the face of a man," is mistaken.

❖ ❖ ❖

Kit Carson

Such stories were told over and over whenever two or more mountain men shared a campfire. Grizzly encounters became almost commonplace, and the trappers who roamed the West were eager to relate their thrilling tales. Most considered the grizzly a formidable and worthy opponent. Some men—like the remarkable scout and Indian fighter, Kit Carson—even admitted that their greatest scares in life had come from a couple of grizzlies.

Carson's near-death experience took place right after he'd downed an elk. Naturally, his gun was unloaded when suddenly, two bears appeared and charged, expecting to chase the man off the kill. Carson ran like the devil, his goal a finger of trees that grew out into the meadow where his elk lay. "I made for them [the trees]," he wrote in his autobiography. "As I got up one of the trees, I had to drop my gun, [as] the bears [were] rushing for me, I had to make all haste to ascend the tree."

Carson shinnied up a stout aspen just in time, with the bears less than a dozen feet away. The man sat perched on a limb until, finally, one of the bears grew tired of the sport and wandered off. The second bear had more patience than the first. He repeatedly flung himself at Carson's tree, huffing and charging and biting at its limbs, yet failed to displace or reach the trapper. Carson later admitted to "never having been so scared in my [entire] life."

❖ ❖ ❖

Joe Meek's Three Close Calls

Grizzlies gave Joe Meek, a young Virginian who had longed for the excitement of the West, more than he bargained for on more than one occasion. Meek was a compatriot of Jim Bridger, Tom Fitzpatrick, and Jim Beckwourth—the brightest stars in the short-lived galaxy that became the mountain-man era. Unlike the tales of both Fitzpatrick and Carson, Meek's encounters with the infamous "white bears" were all provoked.

The most hilarious of all of the trappers' grizzly tales was one that Meek related with great relish. Each time he told it he embellished it further, until no one who heard it ever went away disappointed. One day, Joe and a fellow trapper spotted a big grizzly foraging across the Yellowstone River. No mountain man worth his salt could ever pass up such a hunting opportunity, so the two trappers took careful aim and shot, dropping the animal where it stood. But to prove that they had indeed shot a griz, they knew they had to get enough of the bear back to camp to back up their story.

Now, a mountain man lived for those moments when he might prove, by word or by action, the extent of his bravery. There was never any doubt that these two trappers would cross the Yellowstone River to bring back at least the bear's scalp and paws. They tethered their horses, stripped down to bare skin, and laid their muzzleloaders on the shore. Wearing only their belt knives—how else could they return with their bounty?—they entered the frigid water. They alternately swam and waded across the mighty river and finally emerged on the opposite side. Warily, they climbed up the steep bank and approached the bear just as it shook its massive head and came to its senses. The grizzly rose to its feet, looked at the men, and as Meek later told his biographer, "took after us."

No one, not even a stalwart mountain man, is eager to confront an injured grizzly. The bear was in no

mood for games. It advanced rapidly, closing the distance between itself and the two near-naked trappers,
who bolted for the river. "The bank was about fifteen
feet high above the water," Meek said, "and the river ten
or twelve feet deep; but we didn't halt. Overboard we
went, the b'ar after us, and in the stream about as quick
as we were."

Since their sole hope lay in confusing the bear,
the two trappers immediately swam in opposite directions and finally emerged about a mile downstream
on the same side of the river from which they'd
dived. The bear, which had been properly confused,
swam to the river's opposite shore and promptly took
off for parts unknown, slightly the worse for wear.
The trappers, beaten and humiliated, now had to
walk barefoot and naked upstream to where their
horses were tied. Meek, the consummate storyteller,
probably felt in later years that his humiliation had
been well worth it, judging from the uproarious re-
sponse this tale always received from his audience.

Meek and his companions had another close call
one late-winter day when they came across some
huge grizzly tracks in front of a den in the side of a
mountain. The winter had been unusually harsh.
Meat was scarce in their camp, so one of the trappers suggested that someone go into the cave to drive
the bear out. The trapper, in turn, would be waiting
on a nearby rock so he could shoot the bear when it
appeared. Meek thought this a splendid plan, saying "I'll send old griz out or I wouldn't say so."

Meek didn't have to enter the cave alone; two other
trappers, both eager for glory, joined him. The cave
entrance was so high the men could walk upright. They
moved slowly, allowing time for their eyes to adjust to
the weak light. Imagine their surprise when they saw
a huge bear flanked by two smaller ones standing in

the middle of the cave, staring at them. The three men must have known they were in a heap of trouble.

Yet Meek didn't back down. The bears were apparently bewildered themselves, and this gave Meek a momentary advantage. The trapper edged closer and struck the largest bear with what he termed his "wiping stick." The bear raced right past the trappers toward the cave entrance. As it rushed into the opening, the trapper who had been waiting outside fired a ball into the griz. But the ball missed the vitals, prompting the bear to dash back inside the cave, where the waiting trappers finished it. Then they quickly killed the younger bears. That night, the entire camp feasted on roasted cub meat, a treat at any time, but especially during a long, cold winter.

Meek's most famous bear incident took place along the same Yellowstone River where he had been so ignominiously disgraced a few years previously. Again, he and a couple of companions spotted a large grizzly and her two cubs digging roots on the river's flood plain. But this time Meek hatched what seemed to him to be a well-thought-out plan. He would leave his horse with his companions. They would hold it at the ready while he slipped close to the larger bear and shot it. He felt sure that the two young ones would abandon the scene when their mother fell mortally wounded.

The stalk itself went well, with Meek eventually closing the distance to the unsuspecting bears to a mere forty yards. But when he raised Old Sally (his gun) and pulled the trigger, the cap burst, alerting the bear. No one wants to engage a grizzly in battle at such close quarters, least of all a mountain man armed only with a one-shot muzzleloader. As Meek raced back toward his horse, he tried desperately to put another cap on the gun's nipple. Just as he reached the horses, a melee broke out. All the horses bolted, leaving their

riders clinging to their saddles. By the time Meek's companions got their mounts under control, it was too late
to do anything more for the mountain man.

Meek had managed to get a new cap on his gun.
He stuck the gun inside the bear's mouth and pulled
the trigger. Unfortunately, he'd failed to set it first.
Now the bear was thoroughly enraged. Meek set the
trigger, but before he could shoot, the grizzly hauled
back and gave the gun a swat, knocking it clear of her
mouth. At that moment the gun fired. The bullet hit
the bear but missed her vitals. If Meek had thought
himself in trouble before, it had just tripled. The two
large cubs, seeing their mother attack the trapper, now
joined in the action. The sow knocked Old Sally out of
Meek's hands. The trapper pulled his knife from his
belt. Savagely, he stabbed her behind the ear. But the
bear had had just about enough of Joe Meek. She
reached up with a paw and swatted his knife away, too.

Now the bear was clearly furious. So furious, in
fact, that she began to abuse her cubs. Mother bears
are programmed to protect their young at all costs,
and she was not at all pleased to see her youngsters
at such close quarters with Meek. So while she took
a few moments to cuff her cubs, Meek saw his
chance. He grabbed his tomahawk, his very last
weapon, while he was backed up against a rock ledge.
Meek knew this was it. He would either kill or be
killed. When the griz returned her attention to him,
Meek bided his time. He dodged and parried, trying
to keep his wits about him and his body—particu-
larly his head and the tomahawk he clutched in his
hand—out of the griz's way. He danced around the
bear until at last he saw his opportunity. The bear
presented an opening and the mountain man took it,
slamming the tomahawk with all his might into the
skull behind the great bear's ear. The blade pierced
the sow's brain, and she fell at Meek's feet.

❖   ❖   ❖

A few daring mountain men met their Maker, thanks to grizzly encounters. Andy Sublette, a guide and mountain man who had trapped in Colorado, participated in the Mexican War, and sought his fortune in the gold rush, killed a big California bear in October 1852. The next May he was "shockingly bitten and mutilated" by a wounded bear. Despite his close call, he went hunting at Elizabeth Lake, California, and shot and killed yet another grizzly after it severely mauled him. This bear did its job. Sublette died as a result of his wounds.

Isaac Slover, a trapper who had explored the Colorado River regions with the Pattie party in 1827, went west to California. He, too, lived to a ripe old age. At the age of seventy-seven he still hunted and fished in the San Bernardino Mountains. Perhaps he should have hung up his gun a mite earlier. Slover was killed by a grizzly at the age of eighty-one while traipsing along the north slope of Mount San Antonio.

The mountain men had their hands full when they came up against the grizzly bear. And each brush with death probably served only to burnish the patina of fondness these adventurers felt for the beast they called Ol' Ephraim. While none of us can know for sure, we can imagine the spirits of Joe Meek and Andy Sublette and Broken Hand Fitzpatrick and Kit Carson gathering at the great rendezvous in the sky, where they might be lifting their cups of corn liquor to toast the griz in the finest way they know, saying,

"Them white b'ars—they was some punkins!"

7

Early California Grizzly Attacks

A number of grizzly bear attacks are re-counted in the pages of *California Grizzly* by Storer and Tevis, a valuable reference for any-one interested in learning more about grizzlies. Although many of the most thrilling of these attacks were provoked by men engaged in hunt-ing the great bears, several others weren't.

❖ ❖ ❖

William H. Eddy

One provoked attack occurred on 13 No-vember 1846 and involved William H. Eddy, a member of the ill-fated Donner party. Eddy, who was already feeling the insidious side effects of a slow starvation, cut a huge grizzly track. To Eddy, this track was heaven-sent. The man knew that killing this bear might well mean the difference between life and death, not only for himself but for the weaker members of his starv-ing party. The story begins.

At the distance of about ninety yards he saw the bear, with its head to the ground, engaged in digging roots. The beast was in a small skirt of prairie, and Mr. Eddy, taking advantage of a large fir tree. . . kept himself in concealment. Having put in his mouth the only bullet that was not in his gun, so that he might quickly reload in case of an emergency, he deliberately fired. The bear immediately reared upon its hind legs, and, seeing the smoke from Mr. Eddy's gun, ran fiercely toward him with open jaws. By the time the gun was reloaded, the bear had reached the tree and, with a fierce growl, pursued Mr. Eddy 'round it. Eddy, running swifter than the animal, caught up with it from the rear and disabled it by a shot in the shoulder so that it was no longer able to pursue him. He then dispatched the bear by knocking it on the head with a club. Upon examination, he found that the first shot had pierced the heart.

Despite Eddy's weakened condition, the twenty-eight-year-old emigrant from Illinois helped pack the bear meat back to camp. Most of it was soon devoured. Afterward, the party resorted to boiling hides—including that of Eddy's grizzly—to make a gelatinous soup, which was tasteless but better than nothing.

On 16 December, Eddy accompanied nine other men, five young women, and two boys in an attempt to cross the snow-clogged high Sierra pass below which their party had stalled. Eight days later on Christmas Eve, two male members of the small party died of hypothermia and starvation. What happened next helped ensure that the Donner Party would live on, at least in infamy. Before the men died, they'd urged their companions to eat their human flesh in order to save themselves. Once they'd passed on, a number in the group were driven to do that very thing. Although Eddy held out for several days, at last he too capitulated. The desperate act probably saved his life.

On 17 January 1847, an emaciated Eddy limped weakly into an American settlement on the eastern edge of the Sacramento Valley. His companions had given up hope days before. When a rescue party returned to find those who might still be alive, they retraced Eddy's trail of bloody footprints. Of the seventeen people who had bravely struck out to save the rest of their stranded party just a month earlier, only two men—including Eddy—and the five young women made it out alive.

❖   ❖   ❖

William Kelly

William Kelly met up with a grizzly in Shasta County, California. Although the exact year is unknown, most authorities believe this incident occurred in 1849. Kelly tied up his mule, descended into a gully, and immediately spotted a grizzly bear feeding on manzanita. The man attempted a heart shot, but the ball glanced off the bear's ribs and shattered the animal's shoulder.

The force of this shot staggered the bear, but it quickly recovered its composure. Wounded and with its enemy in plain view, the grizzly charged Kelly. Despite his indiscretion in shooting at the bear, Kelly could hardly be called stupid. He was smart enough to know that he wanted no part of the furious animal. The man raced toward his tethered but nervous mule, leaped into the saddle, and spurred his mount vigorously. With only the lariat to guide the mule—Kelly didn't have time to slip on the bridle—the man had no control over the headstrong animal. The mule stampeded mindlessly, choosing a route that carried him, unfortunately, right under a low-hanging limb. The limb connected with Kelly's solar plexus, stunning the man and flinging him backward out of the saddle. He hit the dirt and leaped to his feet, but it was too late. The bear was on him. Thinking quickly, Kelly drew his knife and stabbed. His swift reaction probably saved his life. When the bear reached out to cuff him, Kelly's blade severed the tendons in one of the bear's great forepaws. With a horrific growl, the bear fell to the ground, blood spouting from the injured paw as if from a geyser. Confused, the bear rose again and upon, finding its paw useless, began to limp around the same tree that had brushed Kelly from the saddle. As the animal circled furiously, it kept its eyes riveted skyward. In anger and in pain, it used its teeth to rip off thick sections of bark. While it vented its spleen on the hapless tree, Kelly finished the bear with a well-placed shot to the back of its skull.

❖ ❖ ❖

Jim Boggs

Jim Boggs met his fate in what was perhaps the most sudden of all early casualties inflicted by grizzly bears. Boggs, who in 1850 was hunting California's Russian River country with two companions, decided to leave them to hunt on his own along a narrow river bottom, the edge of which was fringed with tall timber. The undergrowth in this area was extremely thick, and Boggs's companions, who were hunting the valley's opposite edge, heard their friend shout excitedly. Then, all was still.

> . . . Scarcely three minutes could have elapsed before we reached the body of Boggs, dead and terribly mangled, his entire left side having been torn off by a blow of the bear's paw. His gun, broken within twelve feet of a well used, but now-empty lair, from which the bear had sprung upon him without warning and struck him down before he had time to fire . . . the bear had made off so quickly with her cubs, that we did not get a glimpse of her.

❖ ❖ ❖

James St. Clair Willburn

In October 1857, Trinity County, California, was the site of yet another exciting grizzly attack. James

St. Clair Willburn, a twenty-six-year-old school principal, was earning extra money that year by keeping
gold miners supplied with meat. Accompanied by his
two Indian helpers, Willburn was busily field-dress-
ing several bucks when a grizzly came toward them.
Willburn aimed his muzzleloader and fired, but the
shot was poor. The ball merely creased the bear between the ears and then lodged high in its shoulder.

Willburn now confronted trouble on its own turf.
The grizzly charged, roaring in pain and fury. Indians flew every which way. First, they scrambled out
of the animal's way. When the bear got too close for
comfort, the two men climbed the nearest tall trees.

While the bear was occupied with the Indians,
Willburn grabbed his five-shot, cap-and-ball Navy pistol, hardly a match for an enraged grizzly. The man's
first shot was right on the money, and yet the bear
kept coming. Before Willburn could fire another time,
the bear rose up in front of him, popping its teeth
and growling ominously, and used its tremendous
forepaws to snatch the hunter close. Willburn
shielded his face with his left arm. This gave the
bear ample opportunity to clamp down on it with its
jaws, which crushed the bones like match sticks. As
the bear continued to chomp on his left arm, Willburn
drew his hunting knife from his belt sheath with his
right hand and plunged it deep into the bear's heart.
The grizzly dropped dead at the hunter's feet. Although Willburn recovered, his arm could not be saved.

❖ ❖ ❖

Dr. H.W. Nelson

One hardy Californian even killed a charging
bear with a shotgun. Dr. H.W. Nelson, who prac-
ticed medicine in Placer County, California, had gone
quail hunting. As he trudged through a narrow, brush-
clogged ravine (ravines were deadly in those days),

Nelson heard some men shouting nearby. Their words made his blood run cold: They'd wounded a grizzly bear, and it was headed his way.

> By this time, the good doctor knew escape was probably impossible. So he backed as far as he could into the chaparral and waited, listening to the brush snap and pop as the bear closed in on him. Since his only defense was a shotgun loaded quite inadequately with bird shot, Nelson knew he must make his shot count. He watched in awe as the bear's long strides gobbled up ground. When finally the animal's snout was three feet from the shotgun's muzzle, Nelson fired both barrels at once. The shot sprayed outward, peppering the animal's sinus passages and smashing through the front of its skull. But the bear kept going, knocking Nelson to the ground. The doctor lay with the huge grizzly atop him, afraid to do anything. At last, he realized the animal was dead while he himself was miraculously still alive, although a trifle bruised. The double load of bird shot had killed the gigantic beast while the animal's incredible momentum had bowled Dr. Nelson over, providing him with the scare of his life.

❖ ❖ ❖

The Mendocino Stock-Killing Grizzly

Another thrilling account took place when a group of Mendocino County hunters decided to join forces to dispatch a sheep-killing grizzly. After searching several hours for tracks along a ridgeline trail, the party stopped to eat lunch. They removed their coats and piled them, along with their guns, beneath a tree. They then sprawled out on a grassy hill to enjoy their noonday meal.

According to a lively account detailed in the *Handbook and Directory of Napa Lake, Sonia and Mnemonic Counties* and recounted in *California Grizzly:*

We had just seated ourselves . . . [when] we beheld the largest gentleman of the party, who had just
absented himself from our midst, closely pursued by
a large Grizzly, which had already succeeded in
removing the most necessary portion of his nether
garments [had bitten away most of the man's trou-
sers]. Our ally, the Rancher . . . seized a heavy
stone with which he dealt the bear a powerful blow,
diverting the attack to himself. The entire party now
scattered. . . to avoid the bear and reach the weapons. Meanwhile . . . his Bearship was making rare
sport of our domestic arrangements. At length one
of the party reached the guns . . . and fired. [The
bear] . . . with an angry growl and a slight limp,
denoting the trifling nature of the wound, . . . started
in the direction of the shot.

The rancher ran for his gun: "the bear, smarting
from his wound, and growling ferociously, turned in
his direction," when the man tripped and

was precipitated to the ground . . . Paralyzed
with horror, each stood rooted to the ground, unable to move. Before he could possibly arise, the
bear would be upon him, and one blow from that
powerful paw would end his existence or lacerate
him to such an extent as to render him a cripple
for life. But just as the bear is about to close in on
him, a man without a coat, vest or hat, and showing signs of himself having been roughly handled,
rushes forward . . . Hesitating not a moment, he
throws himself before the prostrate form, and ere
the bear can grasp him, buries his knife in the
animal's heart. With two or three rapid plunges of
his keen knife he finishes the encounter. Both go
down together; the hero and our rescued leader
are stained with the blood of the victim . . . Mr. W.
[the bear's killer], explained that he had acquired
this mode of finishing his game on the occasion of
hunting the boar in Europe.

❖   ❖   ❖

74

John W. Searles

A horrible mauling took place on 15 March 1870 in the mountains of Kern County, California. Fortunately the victim, John W. Searles, survived. Searles was hunting with a number of companions when he heard a bear. He wanted a bear and decided to locate the animal. But the sound had been deceiving. This grizzly was much closer than Searles had thought. It poked its nose high above the brush, not two feet away from where the hunter stood. Searles was thunderstruck, his options limited.

He could not back off because the brush was too thick. He had to do something because by now the bear knew he was there. All he could do was point his Spencer rifle at the beast, pull the trigger, and pray. When Searles fired, his gun was aimed at the bear's jaw, hardly a killing shot. The bear suddenly pitched to all fours and pawed at its burning eyes where flame from the powder had singed its hair. Then disaster struck: Three times more Searles tried to fire, and three times his cartridges failed. Finally the bear rose on its hind legs and opened its mouth menacingly. The hunter saw his opportunity and jammed the rifle between its teeth. But the animal brushed the Spencer aside as if it were a bothersome gnat. It then knocked Searles flat and stood on his chest, pinning him to the ground with one paw. The grizzly reached down and yanked off the man's lower jaw. Then it grabbed him by the throat, severing his windpipe and exposing both the carotid artery and jugular vein. The enraged animal attacked Searles's shoulder, ripping at flesh and muscle until bare joints and bones glistened whitely in the fading light. As Searles lay there, he noticed an arc of blood spurting fountainlike above his face, the result of a severed blood vessel in his shoulder.

As the bear attempted to wrench Searles's arm from its socket, the animal slipped, and the man quickly rolled over. The next time the bear grabbed at him, all its teeth could engage were the thick layers of clothing that had wadded themselves into a ball at the top of the man's back. Disgusted, the bear finally departed.

Searles would have died were it not for the extremely cold air. When his blood-soaked clothing froze, it helped seal the man's savagely torn blood vessels. But Searles wasn't out of the woods yet, not by a long shot. His lower jaw dangled uselessly; his arm hung limp and bloody at his side. But through a combination of sheer will and unimaginable inner fortitude, Searles walked and crawled to his horse and somehow managed to mount it. Clinging desperately to life, Searles rode the four miles back to camp. It took three more days before his companions got the wounded man to a hospital. After surgery, he remained in bed for three weeks.

In later years, Searles derived great pleasure from telling visitors his grisly tale. He would finish it off with details few other grizzly bear survivors could provide: the old Spencer rifle, still dented from the bear's teeth, and a bottle filled to the brim with fragments of his own teeth and bones.

8

Uncle Dick Wootton:
Hand to Hand with the "Big Chief"

The allure of the mountains proved too much to resist for adventurers like "Uncle Dick" Wootton, who was born in Virginia but raised in Kentucky. Wootton was overshadowed by his more famous contemporaries, mountain men such as Kit Carson and Old Jim Baker. The character of the West faded as swiftly as the color in its sunsets, and Wootton changed with it. In time he did it all: trapped, traded, scouted, guided, fought Indians, and hunted buffalo. In his later years he became semi-domesticated and took turns as both rancher and stagecoach station operator.

Frontiersmen like Wootton loved and respected the grizzly. Some admitted fearing the beasts, but few ever backed off upon spotting one. They shared fond memories of the grizzlies' glory days.

Fortunately, before "Uncle Dick" died, he told H. L. Conrad a great deal about his scrapes with grizzlies. Most of these encounters took place in the mid-1800s. Many of them occurred in the Cimarron Mountains just north of present-day Raton, New Mexico. Here are a few of those tales, which were written down by H. L. Conrad in *Pioneer Frontiersmen of the Rocky Mt. Region:*

There was one native of the Rocky Mountain region, which the hunters and trappers always made a point of dealing with very cautiously and circumspectly, and that was the grizzly bear. The grizzly, cinnamon, and black bears were all natives of this region, but the grizzly was the "big chief" of the bear family. There used to be a great many of them in the mountains, but we rarely hear of one now. They have a strong aversion to civilization and have gotten as far away from the settlements as they could get.

I have had a long and intimate acquaintance with the grizzly, and what I tell you about him may correct some erroneous notions which are prevalent as to the kind of animal he is.

In the first place, let me tell you that he is not a professional mankiller and never goes about "seeking whom he may devour," as some writers of bear stories would make us believe. That he has been guilty now and then of staining his chops with human gore is true, but it was usually under circumstances which would have made justifiable homicide a proper verdict if the affair had been between man and man. It was where he met an open enemy in fair fight and got the best of it.

My experience has been that the bear will always sacrifice his reputation for courage to avoid a conflict with the hunter, provided the hunter makes no hostile demonstration when they come in contact with each other.

An experience which I had one time just about forty years ago, when hunting in the Cimarron Mountains, will illustrate to what extent the bear is a peace-loving animal.

Early one morning I left my two companions in camp and started out to get some bear meat. I had not gone more than a hundred yards when I struck the trail of a grizzly, and after following it about a hundred yards farther, through a thick growth of shrub oak which was about as high as my head, I stepped into a little open space and found my bear. I found him in company with four other bears, all full grown.

I was looking for bear, but I hadn't been appointed a delegate to a convention of grizzlies, and I felt at once as though I was an intruder. If I had not attracted their attention, I should have retired without making my presence known or interrupting their deliberations, but they had seen me as soon as I saw them.

I knew that to open hostilities would be suicidal because while I might have killed one or two of the bears, I should have been torn to pieces before the row was over if it had once commenced. It was unsafe to retreat because a bear has no respect for a cowardly enemy, and so I concluded to stand still and give the grizzlies to understand that I didn't propose to commence a fuss.

They eyed me closely for about half a minute, and then commenced growling savagely, first taking a few steps toward me and then walking back to where they started from, as though they were daring me to make any hostile demonstration or even to come half way.

I didn't much like being bullied in that way, but I didn't allow my temper to get the better of my judgment. I stood perfectly still for about five minutes when the bears seemed to reach the conclusion that they had no quarrel with me, and bringing the proceedings of their convention to an abrupt close, they started off on a run in different directions.

I let them go without firing a shot. Their conduct had been much more genteel than I had expected it to be, and I wasn't going to break the peace under the circumstances.

I think they were even more pleased at getting away from me than I was at getting rid of them. One of them at least must have been panic stricken, because he galloped away toward our camp, and when he reached it, was so much excited that he ran through the camp fire, scattering the sparks all over one of my companions, who happened to be roasting a piece of venison at the time.

There is one thing which a grizzly resents very promptly and emphatically and that is being shot at or threatened with a gun. He understands as well as anybody that the gun is a death-dealing weapon, and the snapping of the cap or the click of the hammer enrages him almost if not quite as much as being wounded. Under such circumstances he fights viciously and ferociously without any further provocation.

One of the most desperate encounters I ever had personal knowledge of, between the trappers and a grizzly, was one in which "Dick" Owens, who afterward became somewhat noted as a guide and scout, and John Burris, who, when I last saw him, was a California ranchman, were the participants.

They were out hunting one day and came on to an enormous grizzly very unexpectedly. Both the hunters shot at him and both missed. Before the smoke of their rifles cleared away, the bear charged on them, and they made for a small, bushy cedar tree, hardly more than a shrub, which was the only tree in sight. Owens was ahead and got into the tree, but Burris had hardly gotten off the ground when the bear caught him by one foot and dragged him back. He was a man of rare presence of mind, however, and as soon as the bear caught hold of him, he dropped to the ground, and notwithstanding the fact that his body was being scratched and torn in a score of places, he lay perfectly still.

The enraged bear, thinking he had disposed of one of his enemies, left Burris and climbed into the bush after Owens, who had thrown away his gun and could do nothing but engage in a hand-to-hand fight with old bruin. He struck at the bear with his hunting knife, but the brute caught him by the hand, and then a terrific struggle commenced in the branches of the tree ten or twelve feet from the ground. Burris, although he was badly wounded, had by this time gotten hold of and reloaded his gun, but it was some little time, an age it seemed to Owens, before he could get in a position to shoot at the bear without taking great chances on killing his companion, who was having a wrestling match with the animal in the tree top.

Finally he managed to send a bullet through the bear's body, and the big brute dropped to the ground, almost tearing Owens' hand off before loosening its hold.

This shot was not fatal, but the bear left the two hunters and charged down through our camp, which was not far distant from the scene of the encounter. Several more shots were fired at him, and we finally killed him, but both Owens and Burris were left badly crippled and never entirely recovered.

The hunter who took any unnecessary chances in dealing with a grizzly always regretted it. He always discovered that to trifle with the "monarch of the mountains" under any circumstances was a mistake. Old Jim Baker, who next to Kit Carson was General Fremont's most noted scout, and who has been my companion on many a trapping expedition, used to tell me how he learned this lesson very early in his experience as a mountaineer, and he would always wind up by remarking, "I haint forgot that lesson yet."

Baker came to the mountains about the same time I did, and soon became known as one of the most daring fellows among the mountain men. Two or three years after he came to the country, he and a companion ran across a couple of young grizzlies one morning when they happened to have with them only the butcher knives sticking in their belts. It was not more than a hundred yards to the camp where their guns had been left, but, as Baker said afterward, "I 'lowed we could get away with the varmints with our knives, and we sailed into the fight." Baker had a hard tussle with the bear that he attacked, but finally managed to kill it. Just about the time this contest ended, he noticed that his companion had abandoned the fight, and the second bear charged him without stopping to give him a breathing spell or waiting for time to be called. The struggle which followed between the exhausted hunter and his second antagonist was a desperate one, and poor Baker was more dead than alive when he found himself a victor. He could barely drag himself away from the two ferocious animals that he had slain in close combat, and he never again allowed himself to be inveigled into a rough and tumble fight with a grizzly.

No wonder Old Jim Baker would say with such vehemence, "I haint forgot that lesson yet!" Few men would.

9

The Truth About Grizzly Adams

Executives of the television and motion picture industries have affixed rose-colored lenses to their cameras on more than one occasion. They do so typically when "correcting" the public's perception of what, to them, is a colorful yet totally inappropriate historical figure. One such inappropriate person, at least when measured by today's "politically correct" standards, was John Adams—upon whom the "Grizzly Adams" TV series was based.

Many of us grew up watching Grizzly Adams prowl the TV woods with his pet bear, Gentle Ben. We were entranced as the bear obeyed Adams's every command. But not only was the truth of John Adams's life almost as strange as the tube's fiction, in some respects it was even stranger.

John Adams was born on 22 October 1812 in the town of Medway, Massachusetts. He had a brother, James Capen Adams, whose name he would later commandeer whenever the mood struck him. In later years Adams would occasionally call himself William, but no one knows why. Although young John Adams was apprenticed to a shoemaker, he much preferred working outdoors. He became a top-notch hunter who haunted the forests of New England in search of animals he might capture and sell to a traveling show. After he was injured by one of the show's tigers, Adams briefly returned to work in Boston as a shoemaker. In 1849 he finally abandoned the Eastern shore for the golden promise of California.

When Adams arrived on the West Coast he found work as a miner. Eventually he established a camp in the central portion of the Sierra Nevada mountain range from which he hunted and trapped.

Grizzly Adams was medium in build, according to Theodore H. Hittell, his biographer. He was muscular yet wiry with sharp features and penetrating eyes. In later years he had grizzled gray hair and a white beard. He was partial to buckskin clothing, as were most of the day's active frontiersmen, and wore a buckskin cap adorned with a bushy foxtail.

Adams devoted his life to adventure, and many of those adventures involved bears, his favorite animals. His special relationship with grizzlies began when Adams came upon a sow with two cubs. He killed the sow along with one of its cubs and then lassoed the other with the idea of making it a pet. The surviving cub was furious. It wanted nothing to do with Adams and battled him fiercely until Adams eventually decided to treat the cub as if the man were a bigger, meaner grizzly. From then on Adams combined stern discipline—including beating the cub with a stout club—with a system of reward feeding and punishment. The cub, which he had named Lady Washington, soon had a change of heart. Accepting Adams as a dominant animal, Lady became the man's devoted companion and remained so for the rest of her life. Adams often bragged that his cold camp was much more hospitable when he could snuggle tight against Lady and share in her warmth.

Since Adams purposely sought out bears, he had more than his share of bear scares. Once he was hunting near what is now the border between Washington and British Columbia, armed with only a revolver and a knife. He was accompanied by his faithful Lady Washington, who then weighed about 150 pounds. Adams spotted a deer but got a bad feeling about the place as he suddenly realized it was an ideal spot in which to be ambushed by a bear. He began to back off, but before he could get very far, Lady began snapping and popping her teeth. Turning, he saw a large wild grizzly towering above them on its hind legs. The bear came down onto all fours, moved toward the cowering duo, and then rose in the air again. Adams fired his inadequate pistol into the air, rattled his pet's chain leash, and whooped loudly. That did the trick. The bear scampered for cover.

Adams told many tall tales, but who knows? The way the man lived, many of them were probably true. What we do know is that he was a tremendously gifted amateur naturalist. Grizzly Adams understood, long before any trained biologist did, how a bear's facial expression can reveal much about its intentions. Even more amazing, according to Paul Schullery in *The Bear Hunter's Century*, is that Adams apparently discovered that a bear's age can be determined by the layers of cementum deposited annually upon their teeth starting in their second year of life.

Adams's adventures involved more than just grizzly bears. One day, his Indian companion shot and wounded a black bear. The animal went berserk. Wild with pain, it raced aimlessly around a hillside, ripping up vegetation, almost as if it were searching for the cause of its distress. Adams shot the bear in the chest, but that shot too was ineffective. The animal raced into some heavy cover. Adams went after it, throwing down his now-useless rifle and pulling out both his revolver and knife as he ran.

The bear heard Adams coming. It wheeled and glared at the man. Adams stood his ground until, finally, the bear rushed him. Adams held fire until the last possible moment, then shot the bear at close range in the face, killing the animal in its tracks.

One of the most thrilling accounts of Grizzly Adams's bear-hunting days was this tale, recounted by Hittell.

While in Washington Territory, Adams and his party fell in with three hunters from Texas, one of whom, Kimball by name, Adams had met during his crossing to California. They persuaded Adams to help them hunt, and together they found much game. But one night the camp was invaded by a large grizzly bear that took flight when Adams awoke, saw it, and tossed a hasty shot in its direction. Another of the Texans, a man named William Foster, became agitated about hunting it, almost to the point of rushing after it in the dark. But Adams wouldn't let him. In the morning, however, Adams did lead the three of them in search of the bear. In short order, it was sighted some distance off in company with two cubs.

Adams stationed Foster in a good position to shoot, insisting he not fire until the others reached a nearby hillock, from which they could provide supporting fire. As Adams feared, Foster was too impatient to wait and took his shot while the others were still climbing the hill. The shot was followed by a tremendous roar that, as Adams said, he recognized as the roar a bear makes as it attacks.

By the time Adams had rushed to Foster's aid, it was too late. The poor man had panicked in the face of the charge and attempted to climb a tree, but the bear grabbed a foot and pulled him down, jumped astride of him, and disemboweled him with one swipe of its claws.

. . .The cubs and the sow began to sniff at the dead man, perhaps showing some appetite, so Adams found a tree to steady his rifle against and shot the sow high in the chest. A second shot, in the head, finished her. By then the others had joined him, and five or so of them fired together to kill the cubs, finishing one of them with knives after it did some damage to Tuolumne [Adams's Indian companion]. Foster was buried on the spot.

Adams often remarked that he'd advised Foster, along with everyone else he'd ever guided, to play dead if caught by a bear. Adams believed this was the best course of action to get the bear to leave you alone, proving again how astute were his observations of bears and their behavior.

In the summer of 1854, Adams trapped yet another grizzly while hunting near Yosemite Valley. He named the young male Ben Franklin. In later years Adams described "Gentle Ben" as "the flower of his race, my firmest friend, the boon companion of my after-years."

One day, Adams took Ben and his greyhound, Rambler, along on a wagon trip to his Sierra camp. When they arrived, Adams decided to go hunting. After several hours the trio was making its way back to the wagon when it passed close to a brushy thicket. Adams, who was leading the small procession, was already well into the dense undergrowth when he heard a branch snap loudly nearby. As he turned slightly, a big sow grizzly smashed him to the ground.

Now, Adams was no fool. He was a savvy hunter. The moment he'd heard the branch snap, the man had already started swinging his rifle about. But when the bear cuffed Adams, it not only ripped much of his scalp right off his head, it knocked the rifle from the man's hands. Now the bear really turned on the heat. It lunged toward the stunned mountain man, but before it could do more damage, Rambler latched onto one of its hind legs. With Rambler clinging to the sow's leg, Ben went for her throat. While Adams's two animal friends engaged the surprised sow in battle, Adams crept out from beneath the huge bear, grabbed his rifle, and scurried up a tree. Adams's scalp was hanging down over his forehead and blood was streaming into his eyes. He pushed back the dangling scalp to clear his vision and then made a loud bear screech to draw the animal's attention away from his devoted companions. Adams wanted desperately to save Ben, who was getting mauled badly. Adams knew Ben couldn't last long against a bear the size of the sow. His tactic worked. At the sound of the screech, the sow swung her mighty head in his direction and partially rose on her hind feet to get a better look, and Adams put a ball through her heart. The bear fell over backward, but then her legs began to churn wildly. Adams was afraid the beast would leap back up again so he jumped on top of the sow and finished her off with repeated thrusts of his knife.

Rambler was none the worse for wear. But when Adams turned to Ben all he saw was a blur as the youngster hightailed it back to camp. He found the yearling huddled piteously under the wagon, bleeding badly. Adams knew the smaller grizzly had been grossly overmatched and yet had still sprung to his defense. In gratitude, he treated Ben's wounds before attending to his own, which were considerable. He trimmed the jagged edges of his own scalp, poulticed them with a "decoction of snake root and blood root," and then retired to his cabin. Many weeks would pass before he could leave it. Later, when he checked the she-bear's carcass, he discovered the bear was so old her teeth were badly blunted. Since he was wearing tough leather garments, his injuries were not nearly as bad as they might have been had the bear been in peak condition. The state of the sow's teeth may even have been a cause of the attack since she might have been having trouble finding enough to eat.

Adams never hesitated to take Ben along on hunting trips. The grizzly was so well trained that he'd never touch meat, entrails, or even blood until Adams said it was okay.

Adams became a familiar character on the streets of old San Francisco. He owned and operated the Mountaineer Museum on Clay Street that featured Samson, a giant California grizzly that Adams had trapped. He would wrestle two of his captive bears, straddle their backs, and ride them. He even allowed them to get drunk on whiskey punch because he felt they enjoyed it. The bears liked eating tobacco the best, perhaps because the nicotine stimulated them. But even though Adams's museum did a brisk business, Adams was no businessman. After a few years, he went bankrupt.

Later, he went to work for other entertainment entrepreneurs such as P. T. Barnum. An account in Storer and Tevis's *California Grizzly* described Barnum's first meeting with Adams in April 1860. Barnum's words betray the truth of how difficult Adams's chosen life among his great friends, the bears, had really been:

> During our conversation, Grizzly Adams took off his cap and showed me the top of his head. His skull was literally broken in. It had on various occasions been struck by the fearful paws of his grizzly students; and the last blow, from the bear called General Fremont, had laid open his brain, so that its workings were plainly visible. I remarked that I thought that was a dangerous wound, and might possibly prove fatal.
>
> "Yes," replied Adams, "that will fix me out. It had nearly healed; but old Fremont opened it for me, for the third or fourth time, before I left California, and he did his business so thoroughly, I'm a used-up man. However, I reckon I may live six months or a year yet."

Adams told Barnum that General Fremont was usually so docile, he would use him as a pack animal. But even though Adams's bears were well trained as grizzly bears go, almost every one of them would give the man a cuff or a bite if it had the chance. Adams explained this to Barnum in these words, which were found in *California Grizzly*:

> Mr. Barnum, I am not the man I was five years ago. Then I felt able to stand the hug of any grizzly living, and was always glad to encounter, single-handed, any sort of an animal that dared present himself. But I have been beaten to a jelly, torn almost limb from limb, and nearly chewed up and spit out by these treacherous grizzly bears.

P. T. Barnum was the consummate showman. And in marked comparison to Grizzly Adams, Barnum was also a tremendously successful businessman. Adams begrudged Barnum at least a portion of that success. Apparently, Barnum drove a hard bargain, and Adams was always on the lookout for some way in which he could retaliate for what the old mountain man perceived as past injustices. Barnum himself reminisced about Adams's last great trick after the frontiersman was laid to rest.

> We parted, and he went to Neponset, a small town near Boston, where his (Adams's) wife and daughter lived. He took at once to his bed and never rose from it again . . . The fifth day after arriving home, the physician told him he could not live until the next morning. He received the announcement in perfect calmness, and with the most apparent indifference; then, turning to his wife, with a smile he requested her to have him buried in the new [fringed buckskin] hunting suit. "For," said he, "Barnum agreed to let me have it until I have done with it, and I was determined to fix his flint this time. He shall never see that dress again." His

wife assured him that his request should be complied with. He then sent for the clergyman . . .

Almost his last words were: "Won't Barnum open his eyes when he finds I have humbugged him by being buried in his new hunting dress?" That dress was indeed the shroud in which he was entombed.

According to Paul Schullery, other accounts more reliable than Barnum's substantiate the critical nature of Adams's head injury. In Schullery's words, "It was almost an open wound, a thin layer of skin between the open air and the brain."

The result was inevitable. As Adams had predicted in his conversation with Barnum, after returning home in October 1860 to Neponset, Massachusetts, to his long-suffering wife, he finally died of wounds inflicted by his chosen companions, the mighty grizzlies.

10

A Man-Killing Bear

Theodore Roosevelt was a prolific writer. In *The Youth's Companion*, published in 1893, he related a thrilling bear tale that someone had told to him.

Almost every trapper past middle age who has spent his life in the wilderness has stories to tell about exceptionally savage bears. One of these stories was told in my ranch house one winter evening by an old mountain hunter, clad in fur cap, buckskin hunting shirt and leather trousers, who had come to my ranch at nightfall, when the cowboys were returning from their day's labor.

The old fellow, who was known by the nickname of Buckskin, had camped for several months in the Bad Lands but a score of miles away from my ranch. Most of his previous life had been spent among the main chains of the Rockies. After supper the conversation drifted to bears, always a favorite subject of talk in frontier cabins, and some of my men began to recount their own adventures with these great, clumsy-looking beasts.

This at once aroused the trapper's interest. He soon had the conversation to himself, telling us story after story of the bears he had killed and the escapes he had met with in battling against them.

In particular he told us of one bear which, many years before, had killed the partner with whom at the time he was trapping.

The two men were camped in a high mountain valley in northwestern Wyoming, their camp being pitched at the edge of a "park country"—that is, a region where large glades and groves of tall evergreen trees alternate.

They had been trapping beaver, the animal which, on account of its abundance and the value of the fur, was more eagerly followed than any other by the old-time plains and mountain trappers. They had with them four shaggy pack ponies, such as most of these hunters use, and as these ponies were not needed at the moment, they had been turned loose to shift for themselves in the open glade country.

Late one evening three of the ponies surprised the trappers by galloping up to the campfire and there halting. The fourth did not make his appearance. The trappers knew that some wild beast must have assailed the animals and had probably caught one and caused the others to flee toward the place which they had learned to associate with safety.

Before dawn the next morning the two men started off to look for the lost horse. They skirted several great glades, following the tracks of the ponies that had come to the fire the previous evening. Two miles away, at the edge of a tall pine wood, they found the body of the lost horse, already partially eaten.

The tracks round about showed that the assailant was a grizzly of uncommon size, which had evidently jumped at the horses just after dusk, as they fed up to the edge of the woods. The owner of the horse decided to wait by the carcass for the bear's return, while old Buckskin went off to do the day's work in looking after traps, and the like.

Buckskin was absent all day, and reached camp after nightfall. His friend had come in ahead of him, having waited in vain for the bear. As there was no moon he had not thought it worthwhile to stay by the bait during the night.

The next morning they returned to the carcass and found that the bear had returned and eaten his full, after which he had lumbered off up the hillside. They took up his tracks and followed him for some three hours; but the wary old brute was not to be surprised. When they at last reached the spot where he had made his bed, it was only to find that he must have heard them as they approached, for he had evidently left in a great hurry.

After following the roused animal for some distance, they found they could not overtake him. He was in an ugly mood and kept halting every mile or so to walk to and fro, bite and break down the saplings and paw the earth and dead logs; but in spite of this bullying he would not absolutely await their approach, but always shambled off before they came in sight.

At last they decided to abandon the pursuit. They then separated, each to make an afternoon's hunt and return to camp by his own way.

Our friend reached camp at dusk, but his partner did not turn up that evening at all. However, it was nothing unusual for either one of the two to be off for a night, and Buckskin thought little of it.

Next morning he again hunted all day, and returned to camp fully expecting to see his friend there, but found no sign of him. The second night passed, still without his coming in.

The morning after, the old fellow became uneasy and started to hunt him up. All that day he searched in vain and when, on coming back to camp, there was still no trace of him, he was sure that some accident had happened.

The next morning he went back to the pine grove in which they had separated on leaving the trail of the bear. His friend had worn hobnail boots instead of moccasins, and this made it much easier to follow his tracks. With some difficulty the old hunter traced him for some four miles, until he came to a rocky stretch of country, where all sign of the footprints disappeared.

However, he was a little startled to observe footprints of a different sort. A great bear, without doubt the same one that had killed the horse, had been traveling in a course parallel to that of the man.

Apparently the beast had been lurking just in front of his two pursuers the day they followed him from the carcass; and from the character of 'the sign' Buckskin judged that as soon as he separated from his friend, the bear had likewise turned and had begun to follow the trapper.

The bear had not followed the man into the rocky piece of ground, and when the old hunter failed in his efforts to trace up his friend, he took the trail of the bear instead.

Three-quarters of a mile on, the bear, which had so far been walking, broke into a gallop, the claws making deep scratches here and there in the patches of soft earth. The trail then led into a very thick and dark wood, and here the footprints of the man suddenly reappeared.

For some little time the old hunter was unable to make up his mind with certainty as to which one was following the other; but finally, in the decayed mold by a rotten log, he found unmistakable sign where the print of the bear's foot overlaid that of the man. This put the matter beyond doubt. The bear was following the man.

For a couple of hours more the hunter slowly and with difficulty followed the dim trail.

The bear had apparently not cared to close in, but had slouched along some distance behind the man. Then in a marshy thicket where a mountain stream came down, the end had come.

Evidently, this place the man, still unconscious that he was followed, had turned and gone upward, and the bear, altering his course to an oblique angle, had intercepted him, making his rush just as he came through a patch of low willows. The body of the man lay under the willow branches beside the brook, terribly torn and disfigured.

Evidently the bear had rushed at him so quickly that he could not fire his gun, and had killed him with its powerful jaws. The unfortunate man's body was almost torn to pieces. The killing had evidently been done purely for malice, for the remains were uneaten, nor had the bear returned to them.

Angry and horrified at his friend's fate, old Buckskin spent the next two days looking carefully through the neighboring groves for fresh tracks of the cunning and savage monster. At last he found an open spot of ground where the brute was evidently fond of sunning himself in the early morning, and to this spot the hunter returned before dawn the following day.

He did not have long to wait. By sunrise a slight crackling of the thick undergrowth told him that the bear was approaching. A few minutes afterward the brute appeared. It was a large beast with a poor coat, its head scarred by teeth and claw marks gained in many a combat with others of its own kind.

It came boldly into the opening and lay down, but for some time kept turning its head from side to side so that no shot could be obtained.

At last, growing impatient, the hunter broke a stick. Instantly the bear swung his head around sidewise, and in another moment a bullet crashed into its skull at the base of the ear, and the huge body fell limply over on its side, lifeless.

Had Buckskin's friend had the advantages of either hindsight or an additional century's worth of grizzly bear observations, he might have lived to a ripe old age. When the bear attacked the horse, the two hunters should have realized that wasn't typical grizzly bear behavior, even for the late 1800s. Buckskin's later observation, that the bear had "a poor coat" and its head was "scarred by teeth and claw marks," points to an old survivor, past its prime and doing whatever it could to stay alive. Unfortunately, the trapper understood none of that. That lack of understanding made the man vulnerable, and the bear capitalized on that vulnerability.

11

Richard Wilson:
The Ties That Bind

The frontier could be downright lonely, and into this often-inhospitable environment trekked men who were used to lonely. These were men secure with themselves, and it made sense that they felt most at home with others of their own kind. And yet, ironically, these rugged frontiersmen, loners almost every one, were capable—perhaps more so than most men—of forging lifelong friendships with their comrades. Consider Jim Bridger, a trapper who once bragged he'd gone eighteen years without bread.

After almost two decades in the Rockies, Bridger was nearing his home state of Missouri when he met a group of travelers heading West. "Go with us, Jim," they pleaded. And Ol' Gabe, as he was called by his trading partners in the Shining Mountains, turned his mount's head toward the setting sun with nary a backward glance.

Fraternal love was probably never discussed among these stalwart men. Yet surely it was this type of love that bound them so tightly together. The love and trust that grew between the mountain men and traders, the scouts and cavalrymen, the hunters and cowboys, the men who lived a portion of their lives dependent upon each other, can be compared to that of men who have shared foxholes or active duty in the military. A camaraderie, unshakable and unbreakable, springs up between them, and it may exist, as in a good marriage, until death does them part.

Such was the case with a pair of early Arizona bear hunters. Richard Wilson was neither braver nor more foolhardy than any other man of his time. One day, Wilson decided to take on a grizzly bear. He was alone and undergunned. We might be inclined, from our modern-day perspective, to say he was crazy. Yet consider bungee jumpers and Indy car drivers; free-fall parachutists and stunt pilots. They risk their necks as surely as did the bear hunters and probably for much the same reason: the thrill.

The following account is by Albert E. Thompson. It was first published by the Sedona Westerners in *Those Early Days . . . Oldtimers' Memoirs* in 1968 and was reproduced in part in David E. Brown and John A. Murray's *The Last Grizzly*. Although other versions of this tale vary somewhat, the basic facts remain.

The place? Near Indian Gardens on Oak Creek in Sedona, a locale so busy today it staggers the imagination to think that once it was home to grizzlies and frontiersmen. The year was 1885.

In the words of Albert E. Thompson:

> Mr. Wilson had been telling Thompson [Albert E. Thompson's father] about seeing the tracks of a monstrous grizzly bear between Sedona and Indian Gardens. He said he intended to kill the big bear. He had broken the sight on his large caliber bear gun and had only a small rifle to use. He asked Thompson to take his big rifle to Prescott and have the sights

101

repaired. Thompson told him to leave the big bear absolutely alone until he got back from Prescott with the
big rifle, and the old man agreed to do so.

The evening of the very day that Mr. Thompson left
home, Mr. Wilson failed to show up at the Thompson
cabin in Sedona. Not only did he fail to appear the
first evening, but for eight days Mrs. Thompson and
the two little children, a boy of three and a girl of one
year, were alone. The nearest neighbor was about five
miles away by trail down the creek . . .

On the ninth day she was happy to see two men
riding in on horseback. They were Judge John
Goodwin and his son Tom from Jerome. They asked
Mrs. Thompson for the key to the cabin at Indian
Gardens as they wanted to spend a few days trout
fishing. They were old friends of the Thompsons,
and Mrs. Thompson said she would be glad to let
them have the key, but Mr. Wilson had it. She
told them that she was dreadfully worried for fear
that something serious had happened to Mr. Wilson
or he would not have stayed away so long . . .

The Judge told her that he and his son would ride
on up the canyon and investigate and come back and
let her know what they had found out.

As Mrs. Thompson used to tell it, "They had been
gone for only a short while when I saw them coming
back, riding pretty fast." She knew they had bad news.

They had got only as far as Wilson Canyon. It is the
big canyon that Highway 89A now crosses over at
Midgley Bridge near where it enters Oak Creek. It is
about half way between Sedona and Indian Gardens . . .

The story, pieced out at the inquest and from
what Mrs. Thompson could tell them, is as follows:
Mr. Wilson had quit work early enough in the evening
to get to the Thompson cabin before dark. He had
two pack burros that he had loaded with little pota-
toes for feed for the pigs at Thompson's.

Apparently he and Mr. Thompson had dug pota-
toes previously and packed the marketable ones out
and Thompson had taken them to market in Prescott.

It appeared that Wilson had gotten as far on his way as Wilson Canyon. (Of course, it did not have that name then.) He caught sight of the big bear there. In spite of the fact that he had only a light rifle and a young untrained dog, he could not resist the temptation to kill it. He, an old experienced bear hunter, had lost all fear of the big brutes. He shot the bear and wounded it. Very foolishly he followed it up a brushy canyon with an untrained dog.

It appeared from sign that the bear had gone up the box canyon and stopped in a brush thicket. The hunter followed it by tracks and dripping blood, expecting to get another shot and kill it. He stepped past some Arizona cypress trees, and the bear jumped at him so close he had no chance. He ran for a tree and dropped his gun. He tried to climb the tree, but the bear caught him by the heel of his shoe and pulled him down. He was wearing heavy hobnailed mountaineer shoes. One shoe had the heel almost pulled off and showed the marks of the bear's teeth. The cypress tree that he had tried to climb had a limb almost as thick as a man's wrist and was almost twisted off. It showed how desperately the old hunter had clung to the tree to try to save his life.

The body was found some ten or fifteen feet from the tree. It was lying face down in a little pool of water. It appeared that the bear had pulled the hunter from the tree and either bitten part of his face off or knocked it off with his paw. The belief was that the bear had then gone away. The hunter had regained consciousness and crawled to the pool of water to try to get a drink. He had passed out again and fallen in the water and drowned. At least that is what the jury decided from the evidence at hand.

The old man's body was too badly decomposed to move any great distance. Bedrock was too near the surface to dig a very deep grave. They just wrapped him in his blankets and buried him in a shallow grave and piled a big mound of boulders on top of his grave. At the base of the cliff they cut his initials, R. W., into the rock.

Wilson's partner, Bear Howard, was a giant of a man who stood six feet eight inches tall and was as strong as he was tall. Howard had formed a deep and lasting friendship with Wilson; they'd hunted, farmed, and raised horses and mules together.

Although Mrs. Thompson credits Judge John Goodwin and Tom Goodwin with finding Wilson's remains, some people believe that Bear Howard had really made the gruesome discovery at least five days prior to the Goodwins. According to these accounts, when Howard found Wilson, Wilson's poorly trained black bear hound was feeding on his late master's remains.

Bear Howard went berserk. He became a man possessed, hell-bent on extracting revenge from every bear still able to walk the earth. He trapped and killed bears unmercifully, selling their parts to Asians. Bear Howard died in 1899 at the age of ninety-four with his pet bear nestled at his feet. Finally, after fourteen years, the big man had managed to exorcise his hatred of bears.

The story of Richard Wilson ends with another mystery. According to Albert E. Thompson:

> Some fifteen years after the killing, Frank Thompson, who was a little three year old boy when Wilson was killed, found the skeleton of a very large bear in high brush near the top of Wilson Mountain, some two miles from the scene of the killing. He brought the bear's skull home to his father's house. His father asked him if he had looked for Wilson's hunting knife there. He went back several weeks later but could never find the skeleton again. As it was never found, Thompson always

believed that the old man had stuck it in the bear and the bear had carried it away with him and died from his wounds, but we will never know.

12

Attack on the Rio Colorado Chiquito

Once the Civil War was over, the generals of the U.S. Army, like the mountain men before them, turned their eyes to the West. Violent battles with the now-vanquished South had served only to whet the appetites of many of these men of action. Out there a man could still experience the racing pulse, the quickening breath, that intense feeling of living life to the hilt that comes only in the heat of a fray. Out there Indians still needed conquering, while the wild animals whose meat and hides supported their nomadic ways of life must be killed as well. Out there a man could still be a man.

And so the army went West. Existing forts were beefed up while others were built and garrisoned so that the frontier could be ground into submission. Wildlife of all types provided both food and leisure-time entertainment for the troops. Little thought was given to conservation. With each wild animal killed, Manifest Destiny took a small step closer to becoming reality. When that animal was a grizzly bear, the step was gigantic.

Here is an anonymous account of an escapade that occurred when a group of high-spirited soldiers decided to engage a grizzly in the desert Southwest. It was related by an anonymous author writing in the *Army & Navy Journal*. The date was 12 August 1871:

> On the nineteenth of June last [1871], Captain James C. Hunt, First Cavalry, and Captain W.S. Fuller, Twenty-first Infantry, with five mounted men left Camp Apache, Arizona, for a short visit to the Zuni villages, or Pueblo Indians. The villages lie very nearly 130 miles from Camp Apache, on the road to Fort Wingate, New Mexico, perhaps forty miles from that post. Early in the morning, just after the party had crossed the Rio Colorado Chiquito, on the bank of which they had camped the night before, they passed over an open plain that rose in slight undulations covered with a growth of sage brush and scattering scrub oak. On reaching the top of one of the swells an immense bear was discovered about a mile ahead, evidently coming down the trail to the river for water. The bear at the same moment catching sight of the party turned off to his right, and was heading for the foothills some eight or nine miles distant, as if desirous of gaining the timber. He struck a gait apparently of the clumsiest kind imaginable, but which when tested by the speed of the horses proved that at least for some distance a horse at full speed can hardly keep up with a bear—such ones as we find in the chain of the Rocky Mountains, or the continuations of that range.
>
> By permission of Captain Hunt, Captain Fuller, with Corporal Hyde and Privates Armstrong and Haley, started out their horses to overtake the bear before he could reach the mountains or the rocks and timbers of the foot hills. With horses in good condition, and a free use of spurs, after a chase of four or five miles they succeeded in closing to a few rods distance, or about thirty yards. The party were armed with Spencer carbines and revolvers, with the

exception of Captain F., who carried a heavy Army revolver only. Maintaining a distance of twenty or thirty yards, a lively fire from all was opened on Bruin, but without serious effect. It is not so easy as it may appear to hit an object even of considerable magnitude with carbines or revolvers from the saddle when both the rider and the object fired at are moving at a jump and run, and on rough ground at that.

Captain Fuller by good luck first succeeded in sending a ball through Bruin's hind leg. The effect was to cause the brute to run on three legs, with his right hind leg held off the ground, crimsoned with a free flow of blood. The bear at first rather increased his speed, but the wound soon began to tell on him, as he attempted after gaining a little distance to turn and bite at the wounded foot. A shot from Corporal Hyde's carbine again cut him across the ham. The whole party, keeping up their fire, had drawn up to within some twenty yards of him, when he whirled short round to the left and bounded toward the horse of Corporal Hyde. The corporal turned his horse and gave him the spur, but in a wonderfully short time, considering the clumsy movements of the bear, he overtook the horse and caught him by the flanks. The poor horse gave one desperate kick, for an instant throwing off the bear, but in a second more the horse was pulled down on his haunches, and with one motion of his paw the bear knocked Hyde out of the saddle. The horse galloped off wildly, while the corporal, without any weapons, was rolling on the ground struggling for his life in an actual and literal wrestle with a wounded bear.

It was a desperate position and unequal contest on the ground. Captain Fuller and Armstrong reined in their horses, while within three yards of their horses' feet was this enormous bear ferociously biting and tearing the limbs of the unlucky corporal. The weapons of the party had been discharged and were empty; and with the coolest of men it requires some little time to load a Spencer carbine or revolver while in the saddle. Corporal Hyde struggled manfully, striking with his fists and arms down the mouth and throat of the bear, while his own blood ran in streams from his wounds.

The bear rose twice on his hind legs, standing much above the corporal's head, and the two literally wrestled as two men would in a prize fight. The wounded leg of the bear was Hyde's salvation, or the claws in the brute's hind feet would soon have torn out his entrails. In ferocity and wildness nothing could surpass the horrible appearance of the brute, with bloody foam dripping from his jaws, while the poor man called to the party to help him for God's sake or he would die. No one had a load to fire. Armstrong, believing that there was a load in his carbine, jumped off his horse, and placing the muzzle of his piece against the side of the bear pulled the trigger, but it only snapped. The next instant the bear left Hyde and was tumbling Armstrong, biting and tearing him as he had done with Hyde, who was lying covered with blood a few feet distant. It looked in this position of affairs as if two of the party would receive mortal wounds before the others could assist them. But here Haley got one load in his pistol and fired it at the bear. The ball must have cut him, for he bounded away from Armstrong, and, with his leg held up, again ran for the mountains. The two men presented a dreadful sight, with pale faces, streams of blood running down them, and their clothing torn in shreds. Corporal Hyde only said, "Here is my carbine; kill the damned beast for me, captain, for God's sake!" pointing to his carbine that had been dropped a few yards off when the bear first attacked the horse.

As the rest of the party would soon be up, Captain Fuller and Haley reloaded the carbines, and, having done the best to make Hyde and Armstrong as comfortable as circumstances would admit, remounted and rode after the bear, who was making his way toward the hills, occasionally turning round to lick his hind quarters. The horses, pushed to a run, soon overtook the wounded brute. Riding up to a safe distance, Captain Fuller and Haley fired from their carbines, keeping their horses well in hand to avoid any rush of the bear. After a few shots from each and several attempts of the brute to get at the horses, he turned at bay under a scrub oak, evidently unable to go further and ready to fight. Still the bear's vitality was so great that a dozen more deliberate shots were required, each passing through some part of his body, before his head dropped and he expired.

The conformation of the ground, and the distance ridden in chase of the bear, had concealed these mishaps from the rest of the party, who were greatly surprised at the bloody result of the chase. The bear was of uncommon size, of a brown color, and displayed a boldness and ferocity not credited to that animal by naturalists. The wounds of the men were dressed as well as possible, and with much exertion they were able to reach Zuni villages the second day after the fight.

13

The Tale of Huffman and Shields

William T. Hornaday wrote many thrilling tales of the Old West. In this one, originally published in *Cosmopolitan* in 1887, he recorded the bone-chilling experience of Montana's pioneer sporting photographer, L. A. Huffman, and famous bear hunter G. O. Shields. The story starts as Hornaday visits Huffman in his Miles City studio. The talk soon turns to grizzlies:

"Well now, a grizzly's noble game, and no mistake," stated Huffman. "I'd rather down one old grizzly than a dozen head of any other game. You know, with a grizzly, after the ball is once opened, it's kill or be killed. He's a holy terror, and no mistake. It takes him so long to die, and so much lead to kill him, that he never seems to know when he's got enough. And he's such an all-fired big brute, and so powerful, that if he gets in just one good lick at a man, it's good-bye, John! I tell you, many a good man's been laid low by one blow of a grizzly's paw. It's just like being hit with a sandbag, to say nothing of claws. And what's the worst of it, a grizzly is so tough he'll get up and come at you after he's nominally dead! And very often, you know, a grizzly takes it into his head to do some hunting on his own hook, just when you're not expecting it. They're mighty uncertain in that way. That was what happened after I took that picture" [of an immense bull elk which Hornaday had previously been admiring].

As a prospector would say, I knew I had located a good story, and so determined to have it out then and there. The best way in the world to bring out a narrative is to fire off a whole broadside of leading questions, all in one breath, which nothing less than a complete and circumstantial account will answer. So I said:

"Where did that happen, anyhow, and when? Were you all alone? How did you get into such a scrape, and how on earth did you get out of it? Did you kill the bear?"

"Well, I'll tell you about it, since ye want to know," said the hunting photographer. And as nearly as I can remember them, these were his own words.

It happened up in the Clark's Fork range, near the head of Pat O'Hara Creek. In that neck o'timber you had only to tackle a plum thicket or a chokecherry patch to start up from one to three or four grizzlies. We camped down by the creek and went up the mountains to find elk. Mighty steep the peaks were generally, I tell you.

Well, one morning two of our fellows—Shields and Sawyer—struck a band of elk in a thick fog, up on the side of this peak [pointing to the picture of a snowclad mountain] and killed a cow and a yearling. I was keeping camp that day, so missed that much of the fun.

They were hunting on foot, and, being without packs, of course, could not bring down the meat. What was more, they wanted me to take a view of the game; so Shields decided to stay by it that night, and keep the bears away from it until I could get up to him the next morning with my outfit.

He must have had a lonesome watch; for it certainly was a wild night, blowing and snowing hard. By the way, do you know Shields, G. O. Shields, of

Chicago? No? Well, he is one of the pluckiest and most tireless hunters I ever camped with.

Well, about daylight next morning, as I was rounding up my horses, I heard the bark of his Sharp's rifle, away up the mountainside; and after snatching a quick breakfast, old Ed and I took two packs in tow and started up. The view in the early morning certainly was grand. For a time everything was shut out by the snow and the driving fog, and then suddenly it would lift, and through the breaks we could see the rugged crags and peaks looming up, all covered with snow and ice. When we got within earshot of Shields, he greeted us with a regular war whoop.

"Hooray, old pard!" sezzee. "We've got the chief this pull. He's a ripper, I tell you; big as a beef steer; and horns—oh, hush! Just wait till I take you up to him."

"Where is he?" says I.

"Up the mountain a ways. He came snortin' and blowin' his whistle around my camp just once too often this time; and I'll pack his head to camp if it takes all summer. I blazed the trail as I came down and I guess we can find him without any trouble."

I made haste, and took a view of the cow and yearling—here it is—and then loaded up again, and put some of the meat on my old sorrel. Just then Mike Weise came up; he was a Michigan boy; so taking him along with us, and leaving old Ed to go down alone, we pulled for the prize. It was a long, hard climb and took us until past noon to make it.

Well, it was a grand old elk, and no mistake. No wonder Shields was proud of it! The horns were simply immense. It lay amongst the pines, surrounded by quite an undergrowth of scrub pines and bushes. A few yards below it and a little to one side lay the top of a fallen tree; but, to tell the truth, I didn't notice that until a few minutes later.

As soon as we got there I smelt bear. Do you know you can *smell* a grizzly quite a little distance?

No, I answered, at least not in the woods.

Well, you can. A horse can smell one, too, as quick as a man, if not quicker. I saw then that my old sorrel smelled bear as plain as I did; for he showed it. Sure enough, we found signs of bear on the elk. By Jove! They had pawed the moss and dead branches away from the carcass on all sides and cleared up for a regular picnic. We could see claw marks on the soft parts of the carcass, here and there; and everything looked as if we had put in an appearance just as the first course was about to be served up.

Well, sir, I could smell those bears then just as plainly as I can smell the collodion in that darkroom now; and so could old sorrel. He sniffed and snorted, and peered all about into the scrub pine undergrowth, with his nostrils wide open and his eyes just fairly bulging out. He realized the danger more than any of us men. Finally, I had to take a turn around his nose with a rawhide lasso to keep him from bolting down the mountain. The other fellows didn't seem to feel that there was any danger; but I vow I never felt more skittish in my life.

As quick as I could I began to unpack my view outfit to take a view of the elk, when all of a sudden old Rony, my pet saddle horse, in whom I had all confidence and who had never flinched before, began to get terror-stricken. I tied him, also, then hurriedly made this view of the elk. It ain't a very good one, I know; but you bet I didn't linger very long with my head under that focusing cloth.

As soon as I got my negative I said to the boys: "Now, fellers, if you want to get back to camp with whole hides, you'd better yank the head off that wapiti right lively, for even a bear's patience won't hold out forever. There's a whole snarl of 'em right handy by, and don't you forget it!"

Shields and Mike Weise fell to work right off to skin the elk's neck and cut off the head; and in a few minutes I had my outfit all packed up again. I was standing about fifty feet away from the carcass and rather below it, with a turn of the old sorrel's lariat around my hand. The boys were both bent down over the elk, skinning away, with their back uphill, when all at once, from the scrub pines at a point above us all and between us, out came what seemed to me to be *twenty* grizzlies instead of only three. They were not over forty feet from either of us, and came straight toward me, grunting and "woh, wohing," crowding and snarling, bristles up and mouths open. They meant business, I tell you; but my rifle was on the other side of the elk!

"What on earth did you do?" I asked breathlessly.

Well, siree, there was only one thing I could do. I faced the old bear that was in front, threw up both hands, and bawled out at the top of my lungs, as if I would eat him up: "Hooy! you son of a gun!"

The next instant old sorrel took a flying leap down the hill, jerked me backward through the air as if I had been nothing at all, and we all landed pell-mell in that treetop, horse, man, elk meat, outfit and all, with one tremendous crash.

I was scratched and torn all over; but scrambled out double quick, you bet. The bears had pulled up short; but the boys had not seen them at all, and there they stood, knives in hand, looking at the circus old sorrel and I was making. I yelled out at them: "You blasted fools! Get your guns, and give it to 'em quick, or they'll tear us all to pieces!"

Well, sir, those varmints were so kinder startled by the row, they turned about, "woh, wohing" and snarling, and deliberately walked back into the cover and stopped not fifty feet from where the boys stood.

Weise caught up his gun, and Shields followed suit, while I waved my hat frantically and pointed in the direction of the bears, urging the boys to "get up there and pump 'em full of lead before they make another sally on us."

I tell you, I was scared plenty. Did you ever see an old grizzly stick up his nose and say "Woosh!" to a dog? I had seen that before, but never until I looked up square into that old she's ugly mug had I ever seen or heard anything quite so ugly.

It was Mike's turn next. He made about a dozen or fifteen short, tiptoeing steps in the direction I had pointed, when he suddenly leaped to one side, partly raised his Winchester, and then, without firing, he cleared the distance back to Shields and I in about three of the highest and longest jumps I ever saw a man make.

Right after him lighting right in his tracks at each ump, came an old she-grizzly, crashing through the under-growth, with blood in her eye.

By this time Shields had grasped the situation, and when Mike and the bear broke cover, he stood gun in hand, ready to receive the procession. But Mike showed good pluck. As he landed in the trail near us, he pulled up short, wheeled about, threw his piece to his shoulder, and planted a .45 bullet squarely under the bear's ear, smashing her brains to jelly and killing her instantly. Shields's gun then spoke, and laid another low within fifty feet of us; then rushing a few yards up the hill in the wake of the third one, they sent him into the woods badly wounded.

And then there was such a handshaking as I never saw outside of a revival meeting, and a hurrah that could have been heard in camp, three miles away. We dragged the two bears down to the elk, and fifteen minutes after taking the first picture I made this one. We named it "Elk and Bears: Glory Enough for One Day." Then we packed our trophies, and soon landed in camp, where we had such a supper and such a war dance as I venture to say was never indulged in by palefaces on the Pat O'Hara before nor since.

14

Teddy Roosevelt's Grizzly Tales

The history of North American bears and their attacks is rich with tales told by the men and women who lived them. Some of these characters had numerous run-ins with the beasts. And yet perhaps no one had as many experiences—or at least recorded so many for posterity—as did war hero and eventual president of the United States, Theodore Roosevelt.

T. R. was a true renaissance man. Sickly as a youth, he went west to his Dakota ranch in 1883 hoping to regain his health in the great outdoors. At the same time, an inner restlessness inspired him to learn what he could about the continent's dwindling wildlife species. Gradually, Roosevelt attained a reputation as a fine hunter. Since hunters succeed consistently only after discovering all they can about their quarry, he became one of the country's preeminent authorities on wildlife.

We remember Roosevelt not only for embracing early on the novel concept of conservation. We also remember him for being a legendary trophy hunter. His interest in taking quality animals was so great, it led him to co-found the Boone and Crockett Club, still the premier record-keeping organization of North American big-game species.

A historian once wrote that he felt Roosevelt was driven to prove himself in the "cult of manliness" prevalent at the time. Yet from the late 1880s to the early 1900s, a substantial portion of polite society looked askance at anyone who killed animals for sport. Roosevelt rarely indulged in excessive killing, a fact in which he took great pride. Good sportsmanship and fair play were the credos by which he lived his life. T. R. remained painfully aware of how many game animals lost their lives needlessly to unethical sport hunters, poachers, and the unregulated market hunters of his time. He would not sully himself by doing the same.

Once elected president, Roosevelt's row was extremely tough to hoe. T. R.'s hunting left him wide-open to ridicule from opponents. He became the target of criticism, the subject of intense scrutiny. Then, as now, the press was merciless in its pursuit of stories at the expense of public figures. Roosevelt himself put it best in *The Letters of Theodore Roosevelt,* as edited by Elting Morison:

> I am really at a loss to make up my mind whether it would be possible to take a hunt without having people join us in a way that will interfere with the hunting and without having so much silly and brutal newspaper talk as to leave an unpleasant impression upon the immense number of our people who know nothing whatever of hunting and who accept as true what they see in the press.

During Roosevelt's hunting career he took almost twenty bears. He missed many more. But as he gained hunting skill, he gained a deep respect for bears. This was evident when he wrote to his sister from his

Dakota ranch, "Unless I was bear hunting all the time, I am afraid that I should soon get as restless with this life as with the life at home."

Roosevelt related with gusto many tales of bears and their attacks in writings such as *The Wilderness Hunter* and *The Youth's Companion.* Always, his intense curiosity about bears and why they behaved as they did is clearly evident. He seems to have been sympathetic to their plight and to have envisioned, all too clearly, their diminishing prospects of survival in this selection from *Hunting Trips of a Ranchman*:

> The grizzly bear undoubtedly comes in the category of dangerous game, and is, perhaps, the only animal in the United States that can be fairly so placed, unless we count the few jaguars found north of the Rio Grande. But the danger of hunting the grizzly has been greatly exaggerated, and the sport is certainly very much safer than it was at the beginning of this century. . . Constant contact with rifle-carrying hunters for a period extending over many generations of bear life has taught the grizzly by bitter experience that man is his undoubted overlord, as far as fighting goes; and this knowledge has become an hereditary characteristic. No grizzly will assail a man now unprovoked, and one will almost always rather run than fight; though if he is wounded or thinks himself cornered he will attack his foes with a headlong, reckless fury that renders him one of the most dangerous of wild beasts. The ferocity of all wild animals depends largely upon the amount of resistance they are accustomed to meet with, and the quantity of molestation to which they are subjected.

Roosevelt pursued bears for many years. His constant companions included cattlemen, cowboys, trappers, and hunters. His repertoire of bear stories was huge, and he took great delight in perpetuating them in his many articles and books. Even in his earliest writings, Roosevelt was careful to explain, to the best of his knowledge, why bears acted the way they did. Roosevelt's ruminations on bears became part of the foundation upon which the study of animal behavior was built. Another passage from *Hunting Trips of a Ranchman* provides proof of his fascination with all things "bear:"

A grizzly will only fight if wounded or cornered, or, at least, if he thinks himself cornered. If a man by accident stumbles on to one close up, he's almost certain to be attacked really more from fear than from any other motive; exactly the same reason that makes a rattlesnake strike at a passerby. I have personally known of but one instance of a grizzly turning on a hunter before being wounded. This happened to a friend of mine, a Californian ranchman, who, with two or three of his men, was following a bear that had carried off one of his sheep. They got the bear into a cleft in the mountain from which there was no escape, and he suddenly charged back through the line of his pursuers, struck down one of the horsemen, seized the arm of the man in his jaws, and broke it as if it had been a pipe-stem, and was only killed after a most lively fight, in which, by repeated charges, he at one time drove every one of his assailants off the field.

But two instances have come to my personal knowledge where a man has been killed by a grizzly. One was that of a hunter at the foot of the Bighorn Mountains who had chased a large bear and finally wounded him. The animal turned at once and came straight at the man, whose second shot missed. The bear then closed and passed on, after striking only a single blow; yet that one blow, given with all the power of its thick, immensely muscular forearm, armed with nails as strong as so many hooked steel spikes, tore out the man's collar-bone and snapped through three or four ribs. He never recovered from the shock and died that night.

The other instance occurred to a neighbor of mine—who has a small ranch on the Little Missouri—two or three years ago. He was out on a mining trip and was prospecting with two other men near the headwater of the Little Missouri in the Black Hills country. They were walking down along the river and came to a point of land thrust out into it, which was densely covered with brush and fallen timber. Two of the party walked round by the edge of the stream; but the third, a German, and a very powerful fellow, followed a well-beaten game trail leading through the brushy point. When they were some forty yards apart the two men heard an agonized shout from the German, and at the same time the loud coughing growl, or roar, of a bear. They turned just in time to see their companion struck a terrible blow on the head by a grizzly, which must have been roused from its lair by his almost stepping on it; so close was it that he had no time to fire his rifle, but merely held it up over his head as a guard. Of course, it was struck down, the claws of the great brute at the same time shattering his skull like an eggshell. Yet the man staggered on some ten feet before he fell; but when he did he never spoke or moved again. The two others killed the bear after a short brisk struggle as he was in the midst of a most determined charge.

In 1872, near Fort Wingate, New Mexico, two soldiers of a cavalry regiment came to their death at the claws of a grizzly bear. The army surgeon who attended them told me the particulars, as far as they were known. The men were mail carriers, and one day did not come in at the appointed time. Next day a relief party was sent out to look for them, and after some search found the bodies of both, as well as that of one of the horses. One of the men still showed signs of life; he came to his senses before dying and told the story. They had seen a grizzly and pursued it on horseback with their Spencer rifles. On coming close, one had fired into its side, when it turned with marvellous quickness for so large and unwieldy an animal, and struck down the horse, at the same time inflicting a ghastly wound on the rider. The other man dismounted and came up to the rescue of his companion. The bear then left the latter and attacked the other. Although hit by the bullet, it charged home and threw the man down, and then lay on him and deliberately bit him to death, while his groans and cries were frightful to hear. Afterward it walked off into the bushes without again offering to molest the already mortally wounded victim of its first assault. . .

Last spring, since the above was written, a bear killed a man not very far from my ranch. It was at the time of the floods. Two hunters came down the river by our ranch, on a raft, stopping to take dinner. A score or so miles below, as we afterwards heard from the survivor, they landed and found a bear in a small patch of brushwood. After waiting in vain for it to come out, one of the men rashly attempted to enter the thicket, and was instantly struck down by the beast before he could so much as fire his rifle. It broke in his skull with a blow of its great paw, and then seized his arm in its jaws, biting it through and through in three places, but leaving the body and retreating into the bushes as soon as the unfortunate man's companion approached. We did not hear of the accident until too late to go after the bear, as we were just about starting to join the spring round-up.

Roosevelt had his own close calls while hunting the unpredictable bear that he once had termed, "grisly—in the sense of horrible, exactly as we speak of a 'grisly spectre.'" Strictly speaking, most of these weren't attacks at all, at least not classic, unprovoked attacks. After being fired upon, Roosevelt's grizzlies probably felt entitled to give the hunter a rousing scare. Here is one thrilling tale from *The Wilderness Hunter:*

I spent much of the fall of 1889 hunting on the head-waters of the Salmon and Snake in Idaho, and along the Montana boundary line from the Big Hole Basin and the head of the Wisdom River to the neighborhood of Red Rock Pass and to the north and west of Henry's Lake . . .

For half a mile I walked quickly and silently over the pine needles, across a succession of slight ridges separated by narrow, shallow valleys. The forest here was composed of lodgepole pines, which on the ridges grew close together, with tall slender trunks, while in the valleys the growth was more open. Though the sun was behind the mountains there was yet plenty of light by which to shoot, but it was fading rapidly.

At last, as I was thinking of turning towards camp, I stole up to the crest of one of the ridges, and looked over into the valley some sixty yards off. Immediately I caught the loom of some large, dark object; and another glance showed me a big grizzly walking slowly off with his head down. He was quartering to me, and I fired into his flank, the bullet, as I afterwards found, ranging forward and piercing one lung. At the shot he uttered a loud, moaning grunt and plunged forward at a heavy gallop, while I raced obliquely down the hill to cut him off. After going a few hundred feet he reached a laurel thicket, some thirty yards broad and two or three times as long, which he did not leave. I ran up to the edge and there halted, not liking to venture into the mass of twisted, close-growing stems and glossy foliage. Moreover, as I halted, I heard him utter a peculiar, savage kind of whine from the heart of the brush. Accordingly, I began to skirt the edge, standing on tiptoe and gazing earnestly to see if I could not catch a glimpse of his hide. When I was at the narrowest part of the thicket, he suddenly left it directly opposite, and then wheeled and stood broadside to me on the hillside, a little above. He turned his head stiffly towards me; scarlet strings of froth hung from his lips; his eyes burned like embers in the gloom.

I held true, aiming behind the shoulder, and my bullet shattered the point or lower end of his heart, taking out a big nick. Instantly the great bear turned with a harsh roar of fury and challenge, blowing the bloody foam from his mouth, so that I saw the gleam of his white fangs; and then he charged straight at me, crashing and bounding through the laurel bushes so that it was hard to aim. I waited until he came to a fallen tree, raking him as he topped it with a ball, which entered his chest and went through the cavity of his body, but he neither swerved nor flinched, and at the moment I did not know that I had struck him. He came steadily on, and in another second was almost upon me. I fired for his forehead, but my bullet went low, entering his open mouth, smashing his lower jaw and going into the neck. I leaped to one side almost as I pulled the trigger; and through the hanging smoke the first thing I saw was his paw as he made a vicious side blow at me. The rush of his charge carried him past. As he struck he lurched forward, leaving a pool of bright blood where his muzzle hit the ground; but he recovered himself and made two or three jumps onwards, while I hurriedly jammed a couple of cartridges into the magazine, my rifle holding only four, all of which I had tried. Then he tried to pull up, but as he did so his muscles seemed suddenly to give way, his head drooped, and he rolled over and over like a shot rabbit. Each of my first three bullets had inflicted a mortal wound.

Roosevelt was no fool. Although any hunter who ventured into grizzly country was apt be the recipient of an unprovoked attack, such attacks were, as they are now, fairly rare. Still, he realized that any hunter who deliberately pursued these great bears was treading on dangerous ground. Slipping onto the grizzly's turf, following him into his lairs, and waiting in ambush by carrion for the king of the West to return left Roosevelt convinced of the inherent dangers of hunting the mighty grizzly. He writes again in *The Wilderness Hunter:*

> On the whole, the danger of hunting these bears has been much exaggerated. At the beginning of the present century, when white hunters first encountered the grizzly, he was doubtless an exceedingly savage beast, prone to attack without provocation, and a redoubtable foe to persons armed with the clumsy, small-bore, muzzle-loading rifles of the day. But at present bitter experience has taught him caution. He has been hunted for sport, and hunted for his pelt, and hunted for the bounty, and hunted as a dangerous enemy to stock, until, save in the very

wildest districts, he has learned to be more wary than a deer, and to avoid man's presence almost as carefully as the most timid kind of game. Except in rare cases he will not attack of his own accord, and as a rule, even when wounded his object is escape rather than battle.

❖ ❖ ❖

Dr. James C. Merrill

Roosevelt went on to tell of his friend, Dr. James C. Merrill, who "has had about as much experience with bears as I have had," and who was charged by grizzly bears with "the utmost determination" on three different occasions. In each case, the attack took place before Merrill had even shot at the bear. Although it is difficult to call such attacks provoked, neither can one properly term them unprovoked. One instance, recalled in *The Wilderness Hunter,* was quite extraordinary:

> . . .It occurred in the northern spurs of the Bighorn range. Dr. Merrill, in company with an old hunter, had climbed down into a deep, narrow canyon. The bottom was threaded with well-beaten elk trails. While following one of these the two men turned a corner of the canyon and were instantly charged by an old she-grizzly, so close that it was only by good luck that one of the hurried shots disabled her and caused her to tumble over a cut bank where she was easily finished. They found that she had been lying directly across the game trail, on a smooth, well beaten patch of bare earth, which looked as if it had been dug up, refilled, and trampled down. Looking curiously at this patch they saw a bit of hide only partially covered at one end; digging down they found the body of a well grown grizzly cub. Its skull had been crushed, and the brains licked out, and there were signs of other injuries. The hunters pondered long over this strange discovery, and hazarded many guesses as to its meaning. At last they decided

that probably the cub had been killed and its brains eaten out, either by some old male-grizzly or by a cougar, that the mother had returned and driven away the murderer, and that she had then buried the body and lain above it, waiting to wreak her vengeance on the first passerby.

❖ ❖ ❖

Roosevelt's Tale of Tazewell Woody

One of Roosevelt's acquaintances, Tazewell Woody, hunted the Rockies for thirty years. He killed a great many grizzlies and owed his long life to the excessive amount of caution he always exercised when around them. Woody spoke of his bear encounters at great length with Roosevelt, and T. R. recorded this particular story in *The Wilderness Hunter.*

The only time Woody ever saw a man killed by a bear was once when he had given a touch of variety to his life by shipping on a New Bedford whaler which had touched at one of the Puget Sound ports. The whaler went up to a part of Alaska where bears were very plentiful and bold. One day a couple of boats' crews landed; and the men, who were armed only with an occasional harpoon or lance, scattered over the beach, one of them, a Frenchman, wading into the water after shellfish. Suddenly a bear emerged from some bushes and charged among the astonished sailors, who scattered in every direction; but the bear, said Woody, "just had it in for that Frenchman," and went straight at him. Shrieking with terror he retreated up to his neck in the water; but the bear plunged in after him, caught him, and disemboweled him. One of the Yankee mates then fired a bomb lance into the bear's hips, and the savage beast hobbled off into the dense cover of the low scrub, where the enraged sailor folk were unable to get at it.

❖ ❖ ❖

Old Ike

Roosevelt's perception of bears and their attacks was uncannily accurate for the time in which he lived. He had plenty of experience with bears, for they were still fairly plentiful. Further contributing to his store of knowledge was the close relationship he enjoyed with men who lived and worked in bear country and who had witnessed many attacks. T. R. had seen for himself the ways in which bears trifle with humans. He'd heard of and witnessed the vagaries of attack behavior including serious threats such as bluff charges, dominant posturing, and the pounding of the ground with the forefeet. In *The Wilderness Hunter*, Roosevelt continues his description of what to expect while a grizzly is contemplating attack:

> If a bear means mischief and charges not to escape but to do damage, its aim is to grapple with or throw down its foe and bite him to death. The charge is made at a gallop, the animal sometimes coming on silently, with the mouth shut, and sometimes with the jaws open, the lips drawn back and teeth showing, uttering at the same time a succession of roars or of savage rasping snarls. Certain bears charge without any bluster and perfectly straight; while others first threaten and bully, and even when charging stop to growl, shake the head, and bite at a bush or knock holes in the ground with their fore-paws. Again, some of them charge home with a ferocious resolution which their extreme tenacity of life renders especially dangerous; while others can be turned or driven back even by a shot which is not mortal . . .
>
> Sometimes a single bite causes death. One of the most successful bear hunters I ever knew, an old fellow whose real name I never heard as he was always called Old Ike, was killed in this way in the spring or early summer of 1886 on one of the head-waters of the Salmon. He was a very good shot, had killed nearly a hundred bears with the rifle, and, although often charged, had never met with any accident, so that he

had grown somewhat careless. On the day in question he had met a couple of mining prospectors and was traveling with them, when a grizzly crossed his path. The old hunter immediately ran after it, rapidly gaining, as the bear did not hurry when it saw itself pursued, but slouched slowly forwards, occasionally turning its head to grin and growl. It soon went into a dense grove of young spruce, and as the hunter reached the edge it charged fiercely out. He fired one hasty shot, evidently wounding the animal, but not seriously enough to stop or cripple it; and as his two companions ran forward they saw the bear seize him with its wide-spread jaws, forcing him to the ground. They shouted and fired, and the beast abandoned the fallen man on the instant and sullenly retreated into the spruce thicket, whither they dared not follow it. Their friend was at his last gasp; for the whole side of the chest had been crushed in by the one bite, the lungs showing between the rent ribs.

❖   ❖   ❖

Grizzly of the Freezeout Mountains

Roosevelt was aware of the dangers hunters faced by pursuing a foe as formidable as the grizzly bear. He knew that when following a bear into heavy cover, a hunter could expect it to be lying in ambush for its pursuers. If the bear were already wounded, the hunter's peril was magnified. Again, from *The Wilderness Hunter:*

Most of these accidents occur in following a wounded or worried bear into thick cover; and under such circumstances an animal apparently hopelessly disabled, or in the death throes, may with a last effort kill one or more of its assailants. In 1874 my wife's uncle, Captain Alexander Moore, U.S.A., and my friend Captain Bates, with some men of the 2d and 3d Cavalry, were scouting in Wyoming, near the Freezeout Mountains. One morning they roused a bear in the open prairie and followed it at full speed as it ran towards a small creek. At one spot in the creek

beavers had built a dam, and as usual in such places
there was a thick growth of bushes and willow saplings. Just as the bear reached the edge of this little
jungle it was struck by several balls, both of its forelegs being broken. Nevertheless, it managed to shove
itself forward on its hind legs, and partly rolled, partly
pushed itself into the thicket, the bushes though low
being so dense that its body was at once completely
hidden. The thicket was a mere patch of brush, not
twenty yards across in any direction. The leading troop-
ers reached the edge almost as the bear tumbled in.
One of them, a tall and powerful man named Miller,
instantly dismounted and prepared to force his way in
among the dwarfed willows, which were but breast high.
Among the men who had ridden up were Moore and
Bates, and also the two famous scouts, Buffalo Bill—
long a companion of Captain Moore—and California
Joe, Custer's faithful follower. California Joe had spent
almost all his life on the plains and in the mountains
as a hunter and Indian fighter; and when he saw the
trooper about to rush into the thicket he called out to
him not to do so, warning him of the danger. But the
man was a very reckless fellow and he answered by
jeering at the old hunter for his over-caution in being
afraid of a crippled bear. California Joe made no further effort to dissuade him, remarking quietly: "Very
well, sonny, go in; it's your own affair." Miller then
leaped off the bank on which they stood and strode
into the thicket, holding his rifle at the port. Hardly
had he taken three steps when the bear rose in front of
him, roaring with rage and pain. It was so close that
the man had no chance to fire. Its fore-arms hung
useless and as it reared unsteadily on its hind legs,
lunging forward at him, he seized it by the ears and
strove to hold it back. His strength was very great,
and he actually kept the huge head from his face and
braced himself so that he was not overthrown; but the
bear twisted its muzzle from side to side, biting and
tearing the man's arms and shoulders. Another soldier jumping down slew the beast with a single bullet
and rescued his comrade; but though alive he was too
badly hurt to recover and died after reaching the

hospital. Buffalo Bill was given the bear-skin, and I believe has it now.

Admiration for grizzlies was evident in Roosevelt's choice of words as he acknowledged the bear's great strength, cunning, and fierceness. He often admitted that the grizzly was his favorite game animal, undoubtedly because it was the very embodiment of the qualities he most admired. Yet at the same time, he understood that bears that had been conditioned to the presence of man were quite apt to head for the hills rather than face a confrontation. Roosevelt stressed, in *The Wilderness Hunter*, whenever possible the bears' propensity to bail out of most situations involving humans, even those people who were hunting them. He wrote:

> Ordinarily, however, even in the brush, the bear's object is to slink away, not to fight, and very many are killed even under the most unfavorable circumstances without accident. If an unwounded bear thinks itself unobserved it is not apt to attack; and in thick cover it is really astonishing to see how one of these large animals can hide, and how closely it will lie when there is danger . . .
> On rare occasions men who are not at the time hunting it fall victims to the grizzly. This is usually because they stumble on it unawares and the animal attacks them more in fear than in anger. One such case, resulting fatally, occurred near my own ranch. The man walked almost over a bear while crossing a little point of brush, in a bend of the river, and was brained with a single blow of the paw. In another instance which came to my knowledge the man escaped with a shaking up, and without even a fright. His name was Perkins, and he was out gathering huckleberries in the woods on a mountain side near Pend'Oreille Lake. Suddenly he was sent flying head over heels, by a blow which completely knocked the breath out of his body; and so instantaneous was the whole affair that all he

could ever recollect about it was getting a vague glimpse of the bear just as he was bowled over . . .

❖ ❖ ❖

The Tale of Baptiste Lamoche

Fond as T. R. was of the griz, however, even he had to admit that on rare occasions, they will attack humans for no apparent reason. (However, the following incident may be one of the earliest accounts of a food-conditioned grizzly as reported in *The Wilderness Hunter:*)

I am even inclined to think that there have been wholly exceptional occasions when a grizzly has attacked a man with the deliberate purpose of making a meal of him; when, in other words, it has started on the career of a man-eater. At least, on any other theory I find it difficult to account for an attack which once came to my knowledge. I was at Sand Point, on Pend'Oreille Lake, and met some French and Meti trappers, then in town with their bales of beaver, otter, and sable. One of them, who gave his name as Baptiste Lamoche, had his head twisted over to one side, the result of the bite of a bear. When the accident occurred he was out on a trapping trip with two companions. They had pitched camp right on the shore of a cove in a little lake, and his comrades were off fishing in a dugout or pirogue. He himself was sitting near the shore, by a little lean-to, watching some beaver meat which was sizzling over the dying embers. Suddenly, and without warning, a great bear, which had crept silently up beneath the shadows of the tall evergreens, rushed at him, with a guttural roar, and seized him before he could rise to his feet. It grasped him with its jaws at the junction of the neck and shoulder, making the teeth meet through bone, sinew, and muscle; and turning, racked off towards the forest, dragging with it the helpless and paralyzed victim. Luckily the two men in the canoe had just paddled round the point, in sight of, and close to camp. The man in the bow, seeing the plight of his comrade, seized his rifle and fired at the bear. The bullet went through the beast's lungs, and it forthwith dropped its prey, and running off some two hundred yards, lay down on its side and died. The rescued man recovered full health and strength, but never again carried his head straight.

Paul Schullery's excellent book, *American Bears: Selections from the Writings of Theodore Roosevelt*, focuses intensely on the special feeling Teddy Roosevelt developed for the continent's bears. Anyone wishing to learn more about these fascinating animals at the turn of the century would do well to read it.

15

Besieged by Bears

People have been conditioned to believe that grizzly encounters are bad news. And yet since humans began sharing habitat with these intelligent animals, a few documented cases seem to prove that this isn't always the case. Caution is always called for when watching or photographing bears, or even walking in bear country. But as Enos Mills, the Colorado naturalist, shows us here, not every grizzly bear drama ends tragically. Mills called this tale of an "attack" by three grizzlies the best bear story he'd ever heard. And since he lived most of his life in the Rockies, he must have heard quite a few. This tale was originally told in Mills's account of life in the West, *Wild Life on the Rockies:*

> Two old prospectors, Sullivan and Jason, once took me in for the night, and after supper they related a number of interesting experiences. Among these tales was one of the best bear stories I have ever heard. The story was told in graphic, earnest, realistic style so often possessed by those who

have lived strong, stirring lives among crags and pines. Although twenty years had gone by, these prospectors still had a vivid recollection of that lively night [in the mid 1880s] when they were besieged by three bears, and in recounting the experience they mingled many good word-pictures of bear behavior with their exciting and amusing story. "This happened to us," said Sullivan, "in spite of the fact that we were minding our own business and had never hunted bears."

The siege occurred at their log cabin during the spring of 1884. They were prospecting in Geneva Park, where they had been all winter, driving a tunnel. They were so nearly out of supplies that they could not wait for snowdrifts to melt out of the trail. Provisions must be had, and Sullivan thought that, by allowing twice the usual time, he could make his way down through the drifts and get back to the cabin with them. So one morning, after telling Jason that he would be back the next evening, he took their burro and set off down the mountain. On the way home the next day Sullivan had much difficulty in getting the loaded burro through the snowdrifts, and when within a mile of the cabin, they stuck fast. Sullivan unpacked and rolled the burro out of the snow and was busily repacking when the animal's uneasiness made him look around.

In the edge of the woods, only a short distance away, were three bears, apparently a mother and her two well-grown children. They were sniffing the air eagerly and appeared somewhat excited. The old bear would rise up on her hind paws, sniff the air, then drop back to the ground. She kept her nose pointed toward Sullivan, but did not appear to look at him. The smaller bears moved restlessly about; they would walk a few steps in advance, stand erect, draw their forepaws close to their breasts, and sniff, sniff, sniff the air, upward and in all directions before them. Then they would slowly back up to the old bear. They all seemed very good-natured.

When Sullivan was unpacking the burro, the wrapping had come off two hams which were among the supplies, and the wind had carried the delicious aroma to the bears, who were just out of their winter dens after weeks of fasting. Of course, sugar-cured hams smelled good to them. Sullivan repacked the burro and went on. The bears quietly eyed him for some distance. At a turn in the trail he looked back and saw the bears clawing and smelling the snow on which the provisions had lain while he was getting the burro out of the snowdrift. He went on to the cabin, had supper, and forgot the bears. The log cabin in which he and Jason lived was a small one; it had a door in the side and a small window in one end. The roof was made of a layer of poles thickly covered with earth. A large shepherd dog often shared the cabin with the prospectors. He was a playful fellow, and Sullivan often romped with him. Near their cabin were some vacant cabins of other prospectors, who had "gone out for the winter" and were not yet back for the summer prospecting.

The evening was mild, and as soon as supper was over Sullivan filled his pipe, opened the door, and sat down on the edge of the bed for a smoke while Jason washed the dishes. He had taken only a few pulls at the pipe when there was a rattling at the window. Thinking the dog was outside, Sullivan called, "Why don't you go round to the door?" This invitation was followed by a momentary silence, then smash! A piece of sash and fragments of window glass flew past Sullivan and rattled on the floor. He jumped to his feet. In the dim candlelight he saw a bear's head coming in through the window. He threw his pipe of burning tobacco into the bear's face and eyes, and then grabbed for some steel drills which lay in the corner on the floor. The earth roof had leaked, and the drills were ice-covered and frozen fast to the floor.

While Sullivan was dislodging the drills, Jason began to bombard the bear vigorously with plates from the table. The bear backed out; she was looking for food, not clean plates. However, the instant she was outside, she accepted Sullivan's invitation and went round to the door! And she came for it with a rush. Both Sullivan and Jason jumped to close the door. They were not quick enough, and instead of one bear there were three. The entire family had accepted the invitation and all were trying to come in at once!

When Sullivan and Jason threw their weight against the door, it slammed against the big bear's nose—a very sensitive spot. She gave a savage growl. Apparently she blamed the two other bears either for hurting her nose or for being in the way. At any rate, a row started; halfway in the door the bears began to fight; for a few seconds it seemed as if all the bears would roll inside. Sullivan and Jason pushed against the door with all their might, trying to close it. During the struggle the bears rolled outside and the door went shut with a bang. The heavy securing crossbar was quickly put into place; but not a moment too soon, for an instant later the old bear gave a furious growl and flung herself against the door, making it fairly crack; it seemed as if the door would be broken in. Sullivan and Jason hurriedly knocked their slab bed to pieces and used the slats and heavy sides to prop and strengthen the door. The bears kept surging and clawing at the door, and while the prospectors were spiking the braces against it and giving their entire attention to it, they suddenly felt the cabin shake and heard the logs strain and give. They started back to see the big bear struggling in the window. Only the smallness of the window had prevented the bear from getting in unnoticed and surprising them while they were bracing the door. The window was so small that the bear in trying to get in had almost wedged fast. With hind paws on the ground, forepaws on the windowsill, and shoulders against the log over the window, the big bear was in a position to exert all her enormous strength. Her efforts to get in sprung the logs and gave the cabin the shake which warned.

Sullivan grabbed one of the steel drills and dealt the bear a terrible blow on the head. She gave a growl of mingled pain and fury as she freed herself from the window. Outside she backed off growling.

For a little while things were calmer. Sullivan and Jason, drills in hand, stood guard at the window. After some snarling in front of the window, the bears went 'round to the door. They clawed the door a few times and then began to dig under it. "They are tunneling in for us," said Sullivan. "They want those hams; but they won't get them."

After a time the bears quit digging and started away, occasionally stopping to look hesitatingly back. It was almost eleven o'clock, and the full moon shone splendidly through the pines. The prospectors hoped that the bears were gone for good. There was an old rifle in the cabin, but there were no cartridges, for Sullivan and Jason never hunted and rarely had occasion to fire a gun. But fearing that the animals might return, Sullivan concluded to go to one of the vacant cabins for a loaded Winchester which he knew to be there.

As soon as the bears disappeared, he crawled out of the window and looked cautiously around; then he made a run for the vacant cabin. The bears heard him running, and when he had nearly reached the cabin, they came round the corner of it to see what was the matter. He was up a pine tree in an instant. After a few growls the bears moved off and disappeared behind a vacant cabin. As they had gone behind the cabin which contained the loaded gun, Sullivan thought it would be dangerous to try to make the cabin, for if the door should be swelled fast, the bears would surely get him. Waiting until he thought it safe to return, he dropped to the ground and made a dash for his own cabin. The bears heard him and again gave chase with the evident intention of getting even for all their annoyances. It was only a short distance to his cabin, but the bears were at his heels when he dived in through the broken window.

A bundle of old newspapers was then set on fire and thrown among the bears, to scare them away. There was some snarling, until one of the young bears with a stroke of a forepaw scattered the blazing papers in all directions; then the bears walked round the cabin corner out of sight and remained quiet for several minutes.

Just as Jason was saying, "I hope they are gone for good," there came a thump on the roof which told the prospectors that the bears were still intent on the hams. The bears began to claw the earth off the roof. If they were allowed to continue, they would soon clear off the earth and would then have a chance to tear out the poles. With a few poles torn out, the bears would tumble into the cabin, or perhaps their combined weight might cause the roof to give way and drop them into the cabin. Something had to be done to stop their clawing and if possible get them off the roof. Bundles of hay were taken out of the bed mattress. From time to time Sullivan would set fire to one of the bundles, lean far out through the window, and throw the blazing hay upon the roof among the bears. So long as he kept the fireworks going, the bears did not dig; but they stayed on the roof and became furiously angry. The supply of hay did not last long, and as soon as the annoyance from the bundles of fire ceased, the bears attacked the roof again with renewed vigor.

Then it was decided to prod the bears with red-hot drills thrust up between the poles of the roof. As there was no firewood in the cabin, and as fuel was necessary in order to heat the drills, a part of the floor was torn up for that purpose.

The young bears soon found hot drills too warm for them and scrambled or fell off the roof. But the old one persisted. In a little while she had clawed off a large patch of earth and was tearing the poles with her teeth.

The hams had been hung up on the wall in the end of the cabin; the old bear was tearing just above them. Jason threw the hams on the floor and wanted to throw them out of the window. He thought that the bears would leave contented if they had them. Sullivan thought differently; he said that it would take six hams apiece to satisfy the bears, and that two hams would be only a taste, which would make the bears more reckless than ever. The hams stayed in the cabin.

The old bear had torn some of the poles in two and was madly tearing and biting at others. Sullivan was short and so were the drills. To get within easier reach, he placed the table almost under the gnawing bear, sprang upon it, called to Jason for a red-hot drill. Jason was about to hand him one when he noticed a small bear climbing in at the window, and, taking the drill with him, he sprang over to beat the bear back. Sullivan jumped down to the fire for a drill, and in climbing back on the table he looked up at the gnawed hole and received a shower of dirt in his face and eyes. This made him flinch and he lost his balance and upset the table. He quickly straightened the table and sprang upon it, drill in hand. The old bear had a paw and arm thrust down through the hole between the poles. With a blind stroke she struck the drill and flung it and Sullivan from the table. He shouted to Jason for help, but Jason, with both young bears trying to get in at the window at once, was striking right and left. He had bears and troubles of his own and did not heed Sullivan's call. The old bear thrust her head down through the hole and seemed about to fall in when

Sullivan in desperation grabbed both hams and threw them out of the window.

The young bears at once set up a row over the hams, and the old bear, hearing the fight, jumped off the roof and soon had a ham in her mouth.

While the bears were fighting and eating, Sullivan and Jason tore up the remainder of the floor and barricaded the window. With both door and window closed, they could give their attention to the roof. All the drills were heated, and both stood ready to make it hot for the bears when they should again climb on the roof. But the bears did not return to the roof. After eating the last morsel of the hams, they walked round to the cabin door, scratched it gently, and then became quiet. They had lain down by the door. It was two o'clock in the morning. The inside of the cabin was in utter confusion. The floor was strewn with wreckage; bedding, drills, broken board, broken plates, and hay were scattered about. Sullivan gazed at the chaos and remarked that it looked like poor housekeeping. But he was tired, and, asking Jason to keep watch for a while, he lay down on the blankets and was soon asleep.

Toward daylight the bears got up and walked a few times round the cabin. On each round they clawed at the door, as though to tell Sullivan that they were there, ready for his hospitality. They whined a little, half goodnaturedly, but no one admitted them, and finally, just before sunrise, they took their departure and went leisurely smelling their way down the trail.

16

Timberline Bill's Brawl with a Grizzly

One early grizzly bear attack stands out from all the others because it's documented in a more meticulous fashion than any other. Although this attack was provoked, the incredible details make it worthy of inclusion.

William Sparks, a jack-of-all-trades, tried his hand at prospecting, mining, hunting, cowboying, and packing. He served in Cuba as an officer with Teddy Roosevelt's Rough Riders, and when he returned stateside, he became an Arizona Ranger. Sparks did a turn as a revolutionary, fighting for Cuban independence, and was stationed with the U.S. military in France during World War I.

Today Sparks, who was also known as "Timberline Bill," is best remembered for his writing, especially his book *The Apache Kid, a Bear Fight, and Other True Stories of the Old West*. Here is an abridged version of his true story "A Fight With a Grizzly Bear," which he said occurred in 1888 in Arizona. The action took place near the forks of Eagle Creek at the foot of the Blue Range. The tale vividly illustrates the grizzly's high intelligence and its almost humanlike ability to plan an effective ambush.

The narrative begins with Sparks telling his partner, Al Robertson, that he's going out to check a trap he'd previously set. Sparks first explains how he sets a bear trap:

> . . . When setting a trap for bear, it was the custom to cut a heavy green pole and drive it through the ring attached to the trap until only about eighteen inches of the larger end remained on the side of the ring from which the pole had been inserted. Then, if a bear got in the trap, in dragging the pole through the trees and rocks, he would leave a plain trail and could be easily followed.
>
> But if no pole, or clog, as the hunters and trappers called it, was fixed to the trap and it was left loose, a large bear might travel for many miles before lying up. And if the trap was made fast, when it snapped on a bear's leg it might break the bones, as sometimes happened, and in such a case it seemed to deaden the pain to such an extent that often a trapped bear would twist and gnaw off his leg above the trap and escape.
>
> But this was June; and the bear, as was their habit, had all gone to the higher mountains where there was food in plenty. . .

Sparks concludes that it's too early for bear to be using his trapping area. He then comments that a man from town has requested a lion skin. Sparks decides to trap a mountain lion for this man, explaining that he affixes no clog to the trap when trapping for lion. On the fateful morning, Sparks heads out to check this lion trap. The story continues:

> When I stood over the spot where the [lion] trap had been set, I found that the ground had been almost ploughed up in places by a bear, whose footprints proved him to be a silvertip of enormous size. Different bear, when wounded or caught in a trap, have no

hard and fast rules in regard to their actions. One bear, suddenly finding himself gripped in the torturing jaws of a clattering steel trap, may skulk noiselessly away, while another may frighten all the wood folk within hearing distance with his bawling.

But this bear had acted different from any that I had encountered before. The ground and trees showed plainly where he had swung and struck with the heavy trap, regardless of the pain he must have endured. In places, the trap springs had dug holes in the soil that looked like a shovel had been thrust into it by some careless gardener, and saplings five or six inches in diameter were almost bare of bark in places, where he had snapped and torn with teeth and claws.

The "sign" or appearance of the torn vines and bark, and the tracks, proved that the bear had been caught not long before daylight, and as the sun was now not more than an hour high, I reasoned that the enraged animal would not travel after daylight and might be in any brushy thicket, nursing his hurt, and the hatred that all bear must feel for a trap, and the men who set them.

So I slowly circled around among the trees until I found where the bear, evidently hopping along on three legs and holding the front paw on which the trap was fastened, above the ground, had left the narrow canyon valley, and started straight over a ridge that was covered only with scattered pine trees, and short grass, that made no covering in which a bear could hide.

Though there was no danger of coming suddenly upon the bear here, I climbed the ridge slowly, halting at times to recover my shortened breath. For a rifle is an arm of precision; and the man who has swiftly climbed a steep hill, whose breast is heaving, and nerves jumping from the exertion, cannot pull the trigger with any certainty, as the sights align on a moving or distant target.

And although the bear was encumbered with a heavy trap, I knew that when I came face to face with his bruinship there would be a reckoning on the part of the bear, if my bullets were not sent to the only immediately vital spot in a bear's anatomy—the brain.

The part of a bear's skull that contains the brain is long and almost round, like a curved cylinder in profile, with a thick ridge of bone running from just in front of its junction with the spinal column to below a line drawn between the eyes. The frontal part is thickest beneath this ridge, and as the skull is still very thick, and in grizzlies often covered with several inches of hair, hide and gristle. This was long before the day of high-powered guns, and even the heavy caliber black powder impelled bullets of those days would often glance and fail to penetrate the skull of a large bear, unless they struck it squarely.

But a bullet from a .45-90 that I carried would knock any bear down that it struck in the head; and neither I nor my companion hunters felt the least fear of any bear if we had a few yards of open ground to pump our rifles at him before he could reach us.

It was for this reason that, after reaching the top of the hill, I descended very slowly, always avoiding every clump of brush, and circling around through the openings until I had again picked up the trail, when it went into places where the bear might be hidden. I finally came to the bottom of the hill and a small stream of crystal clear water that gurgled between open groves of small timber. The bed of the creek was sandy, and from twenty-five to seventy-five feet wide. The bear turned directly up the creek, and I followed, still carefully avoiding thickets and turns in the bank where the bear might have laid up for the day. At last I found where the bear had left a thicket and crossed the creek, leaving a string of still wet tracks in the sand; which the sun had now heated so warm that it was evident the bear had heard me, and probably thinking the clump of brush he had laid down in was not so well situated for an ambush as he wished, had silently sneaked away while I was reconnoitering a short distance down the creek.

Presently the tracks led up a gently sloping hill, bare of underbrush, but covered with pine trees. As I slowly neared the top, I heard the rattle of a rattlesnake off to one side, and stepping a few feet toward the sound, I saw a small rattler coiled beside a hole near a large rock. Grasping a small boulder, I flung it at the snake, but missed my mark, and as the snake began to disappear beneath the rock, I hurled missile after missile [sic], but without effect.

When the snake had disappeared, I slowly climbed to the top of the hill, and passing through the open pines, which grew so thickly here that it was slow trailing over the mat of pine needles, I picked up the trail where the bear had started down the farther hillside, which was pretty well covered with scrub oak and buck brush.

I did not follow the trail here, but traveled parallel with it, when I could see it in the soft volcanic ash which covered the hillside, or, when I could not see it, cut across where the course the bear was taking led me to believe it should be, still keeping in the open spaces until I could see the trail ahead of me.

At last I came to a belt of thick brush, and leaving the trail, I skirted this until I came to an opening, which I entered and winding from opening to opening, came at last to a clear space about sixty feet in length, up and down the hill, which at that place sloped at an angle of almost 45 degrees. As I stepped out into this clear space near its upper end I could see the bear's track where he had hopped and slid down through the soft, ashy soil and entered the brush at the lower end of the opening.

Thinking the bear was ahead of me, and holding my rifle in the hollow of my left arm, with my right hand holding its grip, my thumb on the hammer, and the trigger-finger in the trigger-guard, I stepped over into the bear's track just below the fringe of brush the bear had come through. Though I was gazing intently across the gulch, hoping I might see the bear ascending the opposite hillside, I had already chosen my route through another break in the brush just beyond the bear's tracks. As I stepped in the trail I heard the rattle of a trap chain above and behind me, and before I could turn, the bellow of the bear, not unlike the bawl of an enraged bull. I could not turn my feet on the steep hillside as swiftly as my body, and as I tried to face the bear, for I knew there was absolutely no chance for escape by flight, the bear came charging over the brush, snapping at my head, and striking with its unencumbered paw. Both myself and the bear were at a disadvantage on the steep hillside, and attempting to dodge a stroke from the bear's paw, I threw myself to one side and down the hill. As I did so, the rifle, which I had cocked as I tried to turn, was accidentally [sic] discharged, leaving it with the chamber of the barrel empty.

I fell with such momentum that I turned over and over several times, like a boy turning back-somersaults, while the bear, his beady, bloodshot eyes flashing malignant rage and hatred, his ears laid back, and his grizzly gray mane standing erect, tried to check himself as he slid and rolled by me. Snapping like a monstrous dog, just as I stopped rolling, he sunk one tusk, all he had left—he had broken the others off biting at the trap—in my thigh and dragged me along as he slid down the hill.

When bear and man had stopped the bear was standing diagonally over me. The beast's tusk had penetrated my thigh and tore loose a whipcord-looking muscle; and snapping again, the bear caught me by the same thigh. After some effort to balance himself, he rose up on his haunches and shook and swung me like a cat might shake a mouse. At last he slowly came down on his feet, and still holding me in the grip of his great jaws, flung or jerked me until my head lay down the hill, while the bear's rump was up the hill, but his head, his jaws still grasping my leg, was turned almost at right angles toward his right, and my left.

I still grasped my rifle, for there was nothing else to hold onto. As the bear, still snuffing, clamped down again and again on my thigh, I slowly at first, and then with a quick sweep, brought the rifle around until it touched the side of the great brute's head. As I swung the gun, I worked the lever. The bear saw, or heard, and let go his hold on my leg. Just as his head turned and the muzzle of the rifle touched its side, a little below and back of the eye, the lever snapped, my finger gripped the trigger, and the crash and smoke that flamed out told me, even before the bear had fallen, that the scrap was over, for there were still several cartridges in the magazine, and even if the bullet did not reach the bear's brain, it would stun him into helplessness for several moments. But as my right hand jerked the lever and threw another cartridge into the barrel, I saw the bear collapse. His feet seemed to give way under him, and with a sort of convulsive shudder of the muscles, he sank to the ground and rolled over against the brush at the lower side of the open space, just as I, with a great effort, threw myself out of the way. When the bear stopped rolling, he lay on his back with his great paws sticking up and the trap dangling from one of them. Man and bear were not far apart, and as bears have been known to play 'possum, I rose to a sitting position, and poked the bear with the muzzle of my rifle. But there was no doubt that he was dead. A look at the eyes and the great hole in the side of his head where the powder had burned the hair off made that certain.

The bear had evidently heard me throwing rocks at the snake and had circled around through the brush and waited beside his own tracks for his enemy. Had I followed the trail through the brush there can be little doubt I would have fallen an easy victim to the enraged animal. For, as it was, the steep hillside, and loose ashy soil that ran down the hill at every touch of bear or man, was the only thing that saved me.

I now thought of my leg. It felt numb and dead; but I soon found there were no bones broken; but the blood was flowing freely from the wound made by the bear's gnashing tusk. Pulling out my pocket knife, I cut and tore from my cotton flannel undershirt—all I had on except trousers, moccasins, and hat—enough strips to tie a bandage around my leg tightly above the wound. Then, picking up my rifle, I looked again at the magnificent animal that luck alone had enabled me to conquer and limped down the hill to the bottom of the gulch and then on down to where I knew there was an almost ice-cold spring.

When I arrived at the spring, which bubbled up from a small fern-covered cienega, or marsh, I lay face down and drank my fill. Then, slowly limping, I went down the gulch until I came to a place beneath a giant mountain cypress where the bear had dug out a wallowing hole. In spring, when the bears begin to shed their winter coats, they greatly enjoy a mud and water bath, and into one of these wallows I scrambled, not without considerable difficulty. I had observed that although I had tied the bandage tightly above the principal wound—for the broken tusks had done little damage, and the grinding teeth had bruised and not cut—with every limping step the blood spurted out afresh. So, after sitting in the cold water for perhaps twenty minutes, I rebandaged the leg tightly, and finding a dead sapling with a fork about the right size for a crutch, I broke it to the right length. Then leaving my rifle and cartridge belt, I started for the camp.

It was now about an hour before sun down; and I was about five miles from where the trap had been set, and about six and a half miles from the camp. Leaning on the improvised crutch, I limped down the canyon to the creek as I had come. Dark came on, and the rough and narrow fork of the sapling rubbed and chafed my armpit until I stopped and tore most of what remained of my shirt into strips and wound it around the fork of the crutch. Then I hobbled on, hour after hour, through the darkened woods.

Limbs, and vines, and thorns reached out and tore and scratched my exposed skin, but I did not care. I did not think my wound was serious; and while other men of my acquaintance had killed bear in hand-to-hand conflict, none had ever met such a monster as I had—except for the slight handicap of the trap for the bear—fought and killed in a fair fight.

Bear, like hogs, are very heavy for their size. But this bear was larger bodied than a fair-sized cow pony; and although it was June, the season of the year when bear in the foothills are usually poor, he was fat and sleek; a meat-eater that had not gone to the high mountains, but had remained in the lower country to prey on the cowmen's cattle.

Finally I came to the main creek, and stumbling along to the accompaniment of the cries of night animals and birds, wet, weary and sore, came around the point only a hundred yards or so from the camp. Through the trees I could see Al standing by the campfire. At last I crossed the smaller stream and climbed up the bank to the welcoming fire, and the well-meaning but clumsy ministrations of my partner, who finding on his return after dark that the horse he had tied up for me was still unsaddled, knew something had happened but could do nothing until daylight made it possible to follow a trail.

Next morning, long before daylight, Al saddled up and went after the gun, rifle, trap and hide. At that altitude the nights were cold, and he found the skin still in good condition. After skinning the bear, he returned to the camp, and loading me on an easy gaited horse, started for the nearest town, about sixty miles away. That night we stopped at the Double Circle Ranch; the next at McCarthy's Mine, and on the following day we arrived in Clifton, where we sold the bear's hide; and I remained until the wound in my thigh had healed.

17

THE SAD TALE
OF BEAR MOORE

Investigating the historical entanglements between humans and bears of North America involves poring over old newspapers, ancient magazines, and personal letters archived in museum collections, as well as the never-ending search for writings that incorporate such accounts within their pages. Jack Stockbridge's recollections of James A. Moore, which date from the early 1900s, can be found in Elizabeth McFarland's *Wilderness of the Gila.* J. E. Hawley's recollections from the 1920s are reproduced in David Brown's *Grizzly of the Southwest.*

Moore's tale began when he arrived in New Mexico's Gila Wilderness during the early 1880s at a time when soldiers were still busy chasing Geronimo. Moore spent a lot of time in the Mogollons, both camping and hunting, and became intimately familiar with that harsh, unyielding country. Jack Stockbridge furnishes the first portion of James A. "Bear" Moore's grizzly tale and its tragic consequences.

In 1892 I'd [Bear Moore] gone over in the San Mateos to see a friend. I always used one of them old Sharp's 45-70 single shot rifles. About a mile from the cabin where I was staying, I went hunting with that old rifle and I run onto a little young bear up a tree. I shot it but didn't kill it, and it squawked and fell out of that tree.

About that time here comes the old bear. I went to jump back out of the way and fell backwards over a log with the bear right on top of me. As I fell, I lost my gun, but I always carry a bowie knife. Me and that bear had it right there. The bear got a hold of me and bit me through the jaws and on my forehead and through my arms and clawed me across the breast. That bear just darn near chewed me up and spit me out.

I managed to kill the bear with my bowie knife and crawled back a mile to the cabin where my friend was. He taken me in to Magdalena to the hospital and they patched me up there as best they could. My face was left all twisted out to one side and I never shaved after that. I can't talk very plain either. There's scars on my forehead and arms, and you can see my heart beat where that bear clawed my chest open. When I was able, they sent me back to my home in Missouri and I stayed there until I was cured up enough to come back out here again. Ever since, they've always called me Bear Moore."

I [Jack Stockbridge] guess Bear Moore was loco in a way, from thinking about that bear that nearly killed him and left him scarred for the rest of his life. Through the years he kept building bear traps. I found several—half a dozen maybe—around the Mogollon country. He made them out of logs—good, stout logs, some a foot in diameter, I guess. I don't know how the devil the old feller rolled them up together. He would make a trap door out of a big tree he would cut down. The door had to be about three feet wide, big enough for a bear to get in.

I had seen the bear traps around there and I'd heard that he killed the bears—murdered them—in the traps. Once I was going through Little Turkey Park, where Little Turkey runs into Little Creek on the other side of Big Turkey. Bear Moore had a camp there. I heard the durndest racket down in the canyon. I listened a little bit, and it was Bear Moore a-swearing and a-cussing and an old bear growling and just raising Cain. Between them they made a devil of a noise.

I rode down and there was Bear Moore with a bowie knife tied onto a stout stick, poking between the logs of a trap at the bear caught in it. All the time he was cussing the bear. He says, "Oh, you will eat a man up, will you!" and then he'd cuss some more. And he kept on that way until he killed the bear. The bear hide wasn't no good after that—all full of holes.

Albert Pickens and J. E. Hawley were trapping in west-central New Mexico when they heard the bawl of a bear in pain. They slipped closer to see what might be ailing the great beast. When they peered through the trees, they saw Bear Moore torturing a grizzly that was restrained in a cabin trap. Moore had a collection of iron rods he'd heated up in a nearby campfire. He'd then drive them into the bear's body until he killed the animal.

Hawley's account of the beginning of Moore's descent into insanity differs somewhat from Stockbridge's. Hawley said that Moore spotted a large grizzly lurking behind a fallen tree. Moore shot the animal in the back, and when it fell, he was sure he'd broken its spine. But when Moore walked up to the animal, the bear sprang on him.

When Moore didn't return to camp, his partner came looking for him. He found him later that same night. His skin had been ripped away from more than half his face, his jaw had been torn loose, and his beating heart exposed.

Although Moore survived, he was terribly disfigured. He became a recluse and, after fracturing a leg in a remote area, died of exposure during the winter of 1924.

18

Tangling with a Mexican Grizzly

Pushed out of familiar habitats, grizzlies in much of what is now the United States were recently on the verge of extinction. In Mexico, where the great bears also roamed, populations have disappeared. Grizzlies once roamed five of the Mexican states. At one time brown bears could be found in the states of Baja California Norte, Chihuahua, Coahuila, Durango, and Sonora. If remnant grizzlies persist in any of these states, which is doubtful, their best chance of survival would be in Chihuahua's Sierra del Nido.

It was close to here during 1892 that one of the most gruesome of all grizzly attacks occurred. Thanks to Tom Whetten and Ron McKinnon of Tucson, Arizona, George C. Naegle's letter to family members dated 25 June 1892 was reproduced within the pages of David E. Brown and John A. Murray's *Last Grizzly*. Here is that letter:

My dear brother and sister, Joseph and Francis
Toquerville, Wash.

Col, U.T.

This letter will surely be a shock and surprise to
you and the members of our family in Utah and
Arizona, and the pen will but feebly convey to you the
sad intelligence of the fate of our dear brother Hyrum,
who from the horrible wounds inflicted by an enraged
bear, died last night at 10 o'clock. This news will cause
you to feel with us the bitter pangs of grief at his un-
timely death. I now send you the whole circumstances:
Nearly all winter some of us boys have gone to the valley about fifteen miles from here, west, over the
mountain on the Sonora side of the Sierra Madres,
to the ranch. There we would stay the week and
return home on Saturday night. On account of being
so busy, and as father and some of the boys were over
at the new purchase in Sonora, we were usually there
only one at a time to look out for the stock, and especially to save the calves and colts from the bears, mountain lions, and big grey wolves, which have been very
destructive this spring. Already over three hundred
dollars' worth have been lost. Brother Hyrum came
home on Saturday night and said he had encountered
a bear but did not get him. He also reported tracks
quite thick; so we both went over last Monday; on
Tuesday we hunted in different directions, and found
several of our best calves gone. Then we decided to go
together next day down the river Gabalan [Gavilan],
back up North Creek, and gather up all the cows and
calves. I believe that was the first day any of us had
ridden together, the day through, during nearly the
entire spring, and even when two were there we would
ride in different directions, so as to get around among
the stock and over more country. As we came up North
Creek driving a bunch of cattle, on turning a curve in
the canyon and emerging from the point of a hill, Hyrum
exclaimed, "There's a bear!" It was a monster, too.
Instantly we jerked our guns and leaped to the ground.

157

Hyrum had a 44-Winchester and I a 45-70 Marlin. We ran a few paces to a clearing where we had a full view and a fair chance at him. As bruin was going along the bottom of the canyon, Hyrum put in the first shot, and I the next, both hitting him. In rapid succession we fired several shots and I think most of them struck the brute. As he climbed the hill on the opposite side, my third shot brought him rolling and bawling down the hill.

Hyrum said, "that's cooked him," but he only lay a second and gathering himself up, he scrambled to the top of the hill for about twenty or thirty yards and fell under an oak. Hyrum suggested, "Let's take it afoot," and started after him, but having only three cartridges in my magazine, in the haste and excitement of trying to put in more, unfortunately, the first one caught fast, and I could neither force it in nor out until I got my pocket knife. By that time Hyrum was across the creek and climbing the hill, following the bear. I looked up and shouted to him not to follow directly after the brute, but to come in below him, head straight up the hill and come out above or on a level with him. He did so, and as soon as he reached the top, he fired three shots, bang! bang! bang! as quickly as he could. I think the bear must have been on the run while he was shooting, and with the third shot got out of sight over a little raise. In the hurry to adjust my gun and go there I did not look up again till I got the discharged cartridge out and others in. Both Hyrum and the monster being then out of sight, I jumped on my mule—a fleet little animal—and with gun in hand dashed across the canyon. Fortunately I did, for had I taken the journey afoot, I should have reached there too late, for when I arrived on the top of the hill I could not see nor hear anything of them. I called, "Hyrum, Hyrum, where are you?" but received no answer, and sped on the course I thought they had gone but a few rods over a little raise, when I saw the bear above and a little along the hill side, but I could see no Hyrum. Rushing toward the bear, I could see that he had something bloody in his mouth, munching and growling. Not seeing Hyrum anywhere I feared he had him down, and my horror no human tongue can tell when I first saw his blue over-all under the bear's body. He was gnawing Hyrum's hand. I shrieked: "My Lord! My Lord! has he got brother Hyrum." The spurring up of my mule caused the brute to drop the hand and pick up his head. For fear of making an accidental shot and hitting Hyrum, or per-chance the shot might not prove fatal to the bear, I jumped off to make sure aim. Being then quite close, my jump to the ground frightened him, or at least, instead of touching Hyrum again, or making for me before I could level down to shoot, he started off. Hyrum rolled over on his face and rose on his knees and elbows. Then I could see my brother was not dead, but oh! such a bloody sight I am unable to describe. The bear was then about thirty yards from him. I fired and brought the brute to the ground, but he got up and started again. A second shot, however, brought him tumbling again, this time to get up and turn on me; but as he turned he fell, and grabbed in his mouth a dry pine limb about the size of my arm. That he crunched as though it were a cornstalk, and with it in his mouth he started off again. A third shot brought him writhing to the earth, and as my last cartridge was in the barrel, I proceeded within six feet of his head and sent it through the brain of the huge brown bear. I then rushed back to Hyrum. All this was done in half the time it takes to relate.

Now came the trying ordeal for myself. There alone, with Hyrum's mangled body, fifteen miles away from home and help, how I cried and prayed. The poor boy was still resting on his knees and elbows, with the blood entirely covering his head, face and shoulders and still streaming to the ground. The first thing I did was to support his head and administer to him, after which he cried "Water." I galloped to the creek and brought my hat full of water, and washed his head and face the best I could. Such a mangled head and face you never saw. The skull was laid bare from the top of the fore-head about four inches back, and there was one wound on the left side, three-cornered, about two inches each way and one other wound that we did not discover until just before his death, when some portions of his brain oozed out, two teeth having penetrated the brain. On the back and other side of his head, and just at the corner of his right eye, were seven or eight terribly ugly gashes laying bare the skull. There was a long gash down the right cheek and two under the jaw, which was washed; his upper lip was half torn off. In all, there were twenty wounds on his head, face, and the right hand was chewed through and through; his left was bitten through in several places; there was one fearful bite on the left leg, just above the knee, and one heavy imprint of the bear's paw and claws, though not deep, on the right breast. Of course these wounds on his body were not observable at first, but I could see his critical state, and knowing that God alone could help us in our lonely and helpless condition, I told Hyrum to exercise all the faith he had strength to do and I would again administer to him. After this he spoke, and I asked him why he went so near the monster. He said the bear got over a little raise out of sight and was lying down, and he did not see him until within two rods, when the bear sprung up and after him. His gun would not go off, though he kept it leveled on the brute, thinking every second it would act. When the beast was nearly upon him he started backwards, still trying to pull the trigger, but it failed. The bear struck him with his left paw, the right one being disabled, breaking his jaw and knocking him down. The bear then jumped on him, grabbed him by the head with his mouth; and to protect his head and face he put up his hands.

About eight feet from where my brother lay I found his hat and gun. The latter was cocked and contained three cartridges. I think, in the excitement, he failed to press the lever, and that accounted for its not going off.

After tying up his broken jaw and getting him on his horse (which I led), to my astonishment he rode a mile and a half to camp where I laid him upon the bed and washed and dressed his wounds, bandaged them in salt-water cloths and gave him a little milk and cold water to revive him, as he had swooned a couple of times from loss of blood. He rallied and I asked him what I should do—go for help, or try to get him home.

He replied, "don't leave me here alone," and the thought to my self of leaving him while I rode fifteen miles over a very rough trail and returned with help could not be entertained. Again, such a thing as Hyrum riding so far in such a condition could not be hoped for nor expected. But to my astonishment he had, by the help of God, ridden one and a half miles, and I told him that same God, and He only, could give him support and strength to reach home, and if he thought he could stand the ride we would make a start at once. So I quickly saddled him a fresh horse, and provided myself with a two-gallon syrup can of water (which I replenished at Bear Spring), and with a cup and spoon. I put my coat and a slicker on him, as it was cloudy and threatened rain. Then for the third time I administered to him, helped him in the saddle, made a roll of a pair of blankets and a heavy camp quilt to put in front of him to support him, as I though I would have to use these for a bed for him before reaching home. We started at a fast walk, I driving his horse along the trail, he handling the reigns [sic] with his left arm. This went on till dark; then I led the horse through the timber and over the mountain, and by giving him every few moments a little water, which he called for, I arrived with him at his home at 10 o'clock at night, the accident having happened about 3 P.M. on Wednesday, the twenty-second.

In passing through our little town I called up Patriarch Henry Lunt to get others to assist in administering to him and dressing his wounds. I sent for Franklin Scott, his father-in-law, who sewed up the worst of the wounds, and also Sister O.C. Moffatt to assist in caring for him, and we continued from that time to apply every remedy within our reach to allay fever and keep out inflammation, etc. We also sent word to Apostle Thatcher to come and have the doctor from the Carolites sent for. We continued our prayers and supplications for Hyrum's recovery. To all appearance and to the astonishment of every one who saw him, he went on well until yesterday, when about the same time in the p.m. that he was hurt he was taken worse and had quite a bad spell of vomiting. His breathing became heavy and difficult, and the brain began to ooze from two of the gashes in the head. He gradually sank, until just before his noble spirit fled he made a great effort to throw off the accumulation from his lungs. With two or three deep gasps he opened his left eye (which was not hurt) and looked as if to say "Goodbye," and died calmly and peacefully. I think he was conscious to the last, and endured his suffering manfully, patiently, and without a murmur.

To endure such a ride in his condition was char-acteristic of his extraordinarily strong constitution. Not a groan nor a sound did he make while the bear was on him; and not one man in one hundred, per-haps not in five hundred, could have borne what he did without complaint. The grief of those of the fam-ily who surrounded him at his death, and especially the anguish of his young wife was most heartrending. Hyrum was only married in January last. He was 23 and his widow is 19.

I desire to add our gratitude to our Heavenly Father for His tender mercy in bearing him to his home, wife and family; it is a marvel to all how I got home with him. I tell them nothing but the power of God supported him to reach here.

Poor Hyrum has a record in the Mexican mission that will be a monument of honor to him. He was presi-dent of the Deacons Quorum for a while, and was up to the time of his death, an acting priest and one of my counselors in the M.I.A.

I remain, in sympathy and affection, your brother.
Geo. C. Naegle
Colonia Pacheco, Chihuahua, Mexico
June 25, 1892

19

NO LIFE FOR A LADY: AGNES MORLEY CLEAVELAND

As pointed out in previous chapters, human provocation often played an important part in many bear encounters. Typically, a grizzly bear, most often one that had been minding its own business, was backed into a corner and then finished off while it tried to defend itself.

One incident is given an added distinction since it is perhaps the earliest autobiographical account of a woman participating in a grizzly hunt. That woman was Agnes Morley Cleaveland, daughter of a New Mexico ranch owner. The hunt took place in the fall of 1895 when Cleaveland, who was then twenty-one years old, accompanied Montague Stevens and Dan Gatlin on a whirlwind ten-day bear hunt. Stevens, an Englishman with just one arm, was one of the country's foremost bear hunters. He also owned and operated the vast S.U. Ranch, which was headquartered at Horse Springs in what is now Catron County, New Mexico.

The part of the hunt in which Cleaveland experienced the most danger began with this account in her autobiography, *No Life for a Lady*.

We had raced a mile or two following the cry of the dogs, and trying to make shortcuts where possible in order to overtake them. Of the three of us, I knew this particular section best, and was leading out around the skirts of Crosby Mountain, when the one ridiculous incident of the day happened. Dan Gatlin told it later in a saloon in Magdalena something in this wise:

"We was a-ridin' along single file, Miss Agnes in the lead, when we heard a snort up on the mountain above us. We'd woke a grizzly as big as a Missouri mule out of a nice nap, and he was comin' down that mountain with blood in his eye a-hittin' the ground only once't in a while. Miss Agnes she looked up and seen that b'ar and [with infinite scorn in his voice] she run! Then Stevens he looked up and he seen that b'ar and *he* run [more scorn]. Then I looked up and seen that b'ar and [here Dan's voice broke into a high falsetto] *I* run."

My own memory is of a huge dark shape hurtling down the mountain-side directly at us. When finally I succeeded in bringing my horse out of his stampede at least a half-mile away, I seemed to be the only living thing in a vast solitude of mountain range filled with primordial quiet.

There was no bear, no sound of dogs, no Montague Stevens, no Dan Gatlin. Nothing but a quivering horse under me, and a pounding heart in my chest. Which, it seems, was exactly the case in which my two companions found themselves, as we all reported when, after much hallooing back and forth, we got together and compared notes.

From all indications, the bear had been as surprised and as determined to get away as ourselves. Had he singled any of us out for attack, he could have overtaken his victim with ease, for on level ground or in a downhill race, a grizzly can overtake a horse. He lumbers more clumsily uphill but "turns all holts loose" when he starts down. So, a tip to any of you who may go chasing grizzlies: Keep on the uphill side of him.

Feeling decidedly sheepish—for our rout had been completely ignominious, without the slightest claim to presence of mind or bravery on the part of any one of us—we decided to go on in the general direction we supposed the dogs to have taken on the trail of the first bear, the one with the cubs.

Omitting account of one or two tense moments after we finally caught the faint sound of distant baying, I'll bring the picture to the moment when Dan Gatlin and I found ourselves on the edge of a patch of slide rock several acres in extent which lay close under the top of a precipitous peak. It seemed in defiance of the law of gravity that this loose shale remained in place at all. For the first time thus far on the venture, I was downright scared. It just didn't seem possible that a horse could hold his footing at that angle on such an unstable foundation. To have slipped would have meant a plunge downward of five hundred feet.

Dan Gatlin started his horse across it without looking back at me. But somehow I knew that he was aware of my terror, and wanted to reassure me without the injury to my self-respect which mentioning the matter would have involved. He reached into a trouser-pocket, drew out a large claspknife, and began to operate on a fingernail.

"When I git a hangnail," he observed, with what seemed the utmost nonchalance, "I got to cut it off right now."

I still maintain that cowboy chivalry is the truest in the world. Dan Gatlin was to show his again that day. We climbed out over the top of the peak and looked about for Montague Stevens, who had somehow got separated from us. We were now on the north face, and snow lay at least a foot deep, and so solidly crusted it could bear up the weight of our horses. The icy surface made horseback travel impossible, however.

While debating what to do next (I didn't like the idea at all of going back over that slide rock nor yet of taking another step on that ice slide at which we had halted), we suddenly heard the dogs so close that it was startling. The wind until now evidently had been in the opposite direction, carrying the sound away from us. We not only heard but saw them simultaneously.

Far down the mountainside the whole pack was bunched together, yapping on that shrill excited note which proclaims that the quarry is at bay. They were lunging in and out at the base of a great over-hanging boulder.

"She's denned up," Dan Gatlin said, his own voice carrying the same note of excitement. Then he broke into a short laugh [about the incident which happened at the beginning of this story].

"I ain't lost no grizzly bear. If that fool Englishman wants to go on foot a-shootin' of a mad she-bear outen her den, it's all right with me, but far as I'm concerned, I just ain't out no bear."

He was right about it having to be done on foot, if at all. Even that would be perilous over that ice-encrusted snow.

Montague Stevens finally joined us and after a brief survey of the situation decided that he would go down and reconnoiter. He slid from tree to tree, in a series of short tobogganlike dashes.

Arrived at the theater of action, he signaled us to follow. We fastened our horses' bridle reins to the branches of near-by trees and started down. Dan Gatlin carried his rifle. He also had his six-shooter in his belt. Montague Stevens was similarly armed. As I have said, I had no weapon.

Looking back on the idiotic performance, I wonder how three presumably sane people could have engaged in it. Just above the boulder which formed the roof of the bear's den, and a little to one side of it, a Douglas fir sapling stood slim and erect. I was told to climb as high as its branches would sustain my weight.

"Grizzlies don't climb trees," Montague Stevens assured me. "You'll have a ringside seat. I'm going to fire into the mouth of that cave and bring her out. When she comes, you, Dan, be sure you get her before she gets me."

As if this were not madness enough, Dan Gatlin must add to it. Another attack of chivalry had seized him.

"I'll tell you what, Miss Agnes," he said, the light of inspiration in his eye. "You shoot the bear when she comes out. 'Tain't every girl can say she's killed a grizzly."

He passed his rifle up to me.

If Montague Stevens was dubious about this arrangement, he likewise was too chivalrous to make objection. "I'll shoot into the den, then I'll drop back out of range of your fire," he coached me. "When you see her head over the top of the boulder, shoot. You can't miss," he added confidently, whether to reassure himself or me I don't know.

Dan Gatlin stationed himself at the base of another sapling, "just in case." Retelling it later he said, "I clumb and I clumb and I clumb, and when the excitement was all over, by golly, I was three feet off'n the ground."

Montague Stevens shot into the mouth of the cave and leaped back as planned. I had drawn a bead on the spot where the bear's head must appear. But no head appeared. And thereby all our well-timed calculations went by the board.

"By Jove, I must have killed her," said Montague Stevens and took a step forward to peer into the den.

At that instant, the earth shook. Something like a subterranean roar filled the air, and a great dark hulk came out of the den with the momentum of a cannon ball. I was already sighting along the rifle barrel, finger on trigger. Just as I pressed it, it seemed to me that it was Montague Stevens's head and not the bear's which showed in the notched sight of the barrel. Then certainty of it swept over me and turned the world black, for at that same instant Montague Stevens fell and lay absolutely quiet. He had toppled backward over a fallen log and his legs lay across the trunk seemingly lifeless.

Only one who believes he has killed a human being can know the spasm of agony which fairly stopped my heart's beating. Then, somewhere, out of a void of frozen fear, I heard Dan Gatlin's command: "Shoot her agin, Miss Agnes, shoot her agin!"

Mechanically I tried to obey. Ignominious the confession—I snapped the trigger without having thrown a fresh cartridge into the chamber! Then I was aware of

Dan Gatlin at the foot of my tree yelling at me. I dropped the rifle into his hands and threw my arms around the slender top of the sapling's upper trunk to keep myself from toppling to the ground after it.

But Montague Stevens had not been shot. He had accidentally tripped as he sprang backward and was momentarily stunned by the fall. Luckily for him the full dog pack had pounced upon the bear and she had turned to fight them.

I recall seeing the two half-grown cubs standing over Montague Stevens and then I heard the crack of his six-shooter and knew that he was not dead. Relief was almost as great a shock, and I clutched my sapling trunk more frantically than ever.

The mother bear, shaking off the dogs, started around the mountain in one direction, the two cubs in the other. Apparently everybody was at too close range or too excited to have made a direct hit, and in a moment bear and dogs were gone and my two companions were scrambling up the mountain-side to where their horses were tied. I was too dazed to move. I felt unable to unwind my arms from around that sapling's trunk. Rigor mortis itself seemed to have taken possession of me.

I suppose I didn't stay there for as many hours as it seemed. It may have been only minutes; but when I came somewhat to my senses, there was no evidence of life around me, animal or human, and the tree shadows were elongated on the white snow.

Then I recalled the tradition that a mother bear will deliberately, as a protective ruse, run in an opposite direction from her cubs, only to return when she thinks the danger passed to the spot where she left them. I didn't want that bear to come back and find me up as inadequate a tree as that sapling. I slid to the ground and began to climb the icy slope to my horse. At every step I felt the bear's hot breath upon me. Imagination had broken through all barriers of reason; I was just a badly scared girl in an awesome setting. The north side of Crosby Mountain at twilight, with the suggestion of grizzlies at every turn, may, I think, without exaggeration be termed awesome.

Gasping with exhaustion, my lungs on fire from the effort of trying to run up an icy mountain-side at an altitude of ten thousand feet, I finally reached the place where I had tied my horse.

He was not there. A broken branch was evidence of his having jerked loose, presumably when the other horses left with the two men on them. Two courses lay before me, to collapse in sheer panic and freeze to death, or to gather myself together. I made an effort in the latter direction. I'd asked for this, hadn't I? I'd been warned that bear-hunting wasn't a chivalrous pursuit. Was I to whimper now that the warning had become reality?

I'd never been eaten by a bear yet, I assured myself, and the chances were I wouldn't be! I set out on my horse's well-defined trail. The fragment of limb which dragged from the bridle rein had left a clear scratch in the snow that could be followed rapidly, so long as daylight lasted. I overtook him just before the shadows deepened into utter blackness.

The nearest ranch was the JL and I headed for it. The horse had found an easier descent from the peak than the way we climbed up, and by the time I caught him we were well down on the relatively gentler slopes. An hour's ride brought me to the JL Ranch and a surprised welcome.

Montague Stevens came in later with the dogs and no bear. He had seen neither mother nor cubs again. It was after daylight when Dan Gatlin arrived, reporting still another bear jumped and killed by another of those miraculous shots of his.

Remember, Montague Stevens had but one arm. But he has probably more bear to his credit than any man living, unless it be professional hunters. It was the next season that he killed the bear who was, so I insist, the famous Big Susie.

Actually, according to Stevens's own account in his book *Meet Mr. Grizzly*, he finally killed the grizzly he'd nicknamed Susie three years later. When he did so, after a long chase on horseback to the baying of his bear hounds, Stevens wrote:

170

The defeat of Susie was the red-letter day of all my hunting experiences. It marked the gratifying culmination of years of hard work and painstaking mental effort, and proved that bloodhounds could be trained to trail any animal successfully, without having had any previous experience in hunting that particular animal.

20

Utah's Old Ephraim

This tale of a provoked grizzly bear attack deserves inclusion for two reasons. First, it is one of only two accounts in this book of an attack by a stock-killing grizzly; second, the subject has become a legend— Old Ephraim, Utah's last grizzly.

❖ ❖ ❖

By 1923 Old Ephraim, a notorious stock-killing grizzly, had become not only a Wasatch Mountain legend, he was also Utah's last grizzly. No one mourned the passing of the final symbol of what once had been a wilderness as impenetrable as night. No one seemed to care at all, for Ephraim was a stock marauder. He threatened men's livelihoods, so he had to be destroyed. Trouble was, many men had tried, and many men had failed. But on 22 August Frank Clark from Malad, Idaho, a most unlikely bear slayer, finally brought down the giant bear. Clark won, but most of his contemporaries swore that he regretted what he'd done until his dying day.

Our story begins soon after Clark and his partner, Frank Kemp, had established a sheep camp near the head of Rick's Canyon. Clark remembered when grizzly bears had been numerous in these mountains. He'd listened to tales of the mountain men who wintered in nearby Cache Valley and pondered how they'd kept themselves warm in hides taken from the once-plentiful bears, and he knew they'd measured their wealth in the many luxurious pelts and gallons of rich bear oil they would trade at summer rendezvous.

As Clark stood high atop the mountains surrounding his sheep range, he could see miles of meandering streams threading their way across Cache Valley. He knew these waters would keep moving until they reached the vast and mysterious sea. He saw the graceful willows that clung to the banks of both waterway and beaver pond. And he could also see evidence of how settlers had pushed back the wilderness, taming and cultivating what had once been desolation.

The settlers could not exist peaceably with the grizzly. Clark knew that any bear bold enough to let itself or its tracks be seen would quickly have been hunted down and killed. Now, in the early years of the century, both bears and frontier had long since faded into history. All except Old Ephraim.

❖　❖　❖

Plenty of mountain men had called this bear or that one by the name "Old Ephraim." It was simply a name from Scripture well suited to the regal old king of the mountains. What made this Old Ephraim different from all the other Old Ephraims that had preceded him was his delight in killing sheep. That, and the fact that this Old Ephraim was Utah's last grizzly.

Sheepmen could identify Old Ephraim by his distinctive hind track: 12 inches long, not counting claws, and missing the middle claw on the left foot.

Old Ephraim traveled the territory between Bear Lake and the head of Ogden Canyon. This was the old patriarch's home range, and he was loathe to leave it. Ephraim was cunning; often, he would plunder sheep in one corner of his territory and then move elsewhere and stir up trouble there as well.

Soon the stockmen began joshing each other, sending postcards that predicted Ephraim's reappearance in another area. "Ephraim will soon be visiting your mutton," one would read, and before too long, visions of the bear permeated the dreams and imaginations of almost everyone in the area.

Ephraim was wily. The animal was deserving of his growing legend, on a par with California's legendary stock-killing bears: Old Clubfoot, Old Bruno, Three-Toes, and Big Bear. Many an attempt was made to trap and kill Ephraim for he was, after all, the last of his kind, and once he was gone the country would be safe. Yet Old Ephraim consistently evaded the humans who pursued him. The only real evidence that the bear even existed was his kills and his distinctive tracks.

In the summer of 1923, Clark and Kemp were grazing sheep in the country beyond Rick's Canyon. Other sheepherders had used the area before but had always bailed out because of bear trouble. But these two men were range-tough. They aggressively pursued any sheep-killing bears that crossed their paths. In twelve years they'd trapped and dispatched twenty-two black bears. Clark and Kemp were feeling pretty smug that summer of 1923. They knew of Old Ephraim, but as long as he left their stock alone, he'd get no quarrel from them.

One day in late August, Kemp was tending the sheep. The sun was warm and the man grew sleepy. He dozed off as he slouched down against a rotting log in a small, grassy meadow. Suddenly, the hair stood up on the back of Kemp's neck. The man felt something staring at him, but what, he didn't know. He turned, moving slowly. Standing a short distance behind him, looking his way, was the largest bear Kemp had ever seen. The bear didn't appear to be concerned. It sniffed the air and trundled slowly back into the aspens. Kemp waited a moment, stumbled to his feet, and hurried back to camp. He told Clark what he'd seen. The two men knew that the bear was probably Old Ephraim. They decided to investigate further.

They returned to the spot where Kemp had seen the bear. From there they spread out and soon found large tracks heading into the timber, huge tracks with no middle claw on the left hind foot. Old Ephraim! They whispered together excitedly, not sure what to do next. Finally they decided to track the bear. They followed its tracks into the aspens until they reached a sunken area where a wet-weather spring had thoroughly saturated the earth. It was obvious that the grizzly spent a lot of time here, wallowing away the hot summer hours in the damp, refreshing mud. What was so incredible was that they'd been camped nearby for weeks without ever suspecting that the griz was anywhere close. They concocted a plan: They would try to trap the bear here, where he spent so much time.

Clark raced back to camp. When he returned he was carrying a heavy bear trap. He walked closer to the wallow, chained the trap to a cumbersome drag pole, and pulled its jaws apart. Before he left, he erased all evidence of the men having been there.

Clark returned two days later. He was filled with anxiety, wondering if Old Ephraim had wandered into his trap. He learned the answer quickly: The trap had been dug up and placed neatly alongside the drag log. The bear had been so careful, the trap was in the upright position and hadn't even been sprung! Old Ephraim had accepted Clark's challenge.

From then on, Clark knew the issue would be resolved only when one of them emerged as the clear victor. And at that point, Clark had no idea who that might be. He hoped it would be him, yet he knew Old Ephraim had trifled with far better men of the mountains and had managed to keep his hide. Yet Clark was not deterred. He just decided he'd do his best and let the chips fall where they might.

Clark set the trap again. A few days later, Old Ephraim dug it up again, leaving it unsprung where Clark was bound to see it. Clark grinned. Each time he'd set the trap on a hair trigger. The big bear, he thought, must be exceedingly deft to dig up and move such a heavy trap without springing it.

Old Ephraim had demonstrated how smart he truly was. And while the man had persisted in setting the trap near the bear's favorite wallow, the bear had determined that nothing—not even a trap—would keep him from using the mud hole. But Old Ephraim knew traps were dangerous. So the bear created a new wallow by scratching a channel into the ground that would carry spring water from the original wallow to a new sink. From the sign left behind, Clark knew Ephraim was using his new wallow to his heart's content with no fear that a hidden trap would spring on him.

Cursing to himself, the sheepherder fetched a second trap. This time, he positioned one trap in the bear's new wallow and buried the second trap at its edge.

That night Clark camped nearby. He had trouble getting to sleep, for he knew the legendary grizzly must be prowling nearby. His only insurance was the gun and the stash of extra cartridges he kept close at hand.

He must have dozed off, because the next thing he knew, he was staring at a darkened sky. Clark waited, unsure what had awakened him, when suddenly an unearthly noise, a wild moaning, jolted him from his bedroll. A thunderous groan bellowed through the meadow, followed by the distinct clanking of metal on metal. Never had the man heard such a horrible sound. He pulled on his boots, seized his rifle, and slipped through the sagebrush toward the sound. He'd set the traps quite a distance from where he now heard the wild roaring. The only explanation was that the bear was headed this way, dragging the hated trap and drag log behind him.

Clark gripped the rifle tighter and checked to be certain he'd loaded a cartridge in its chamber. He cocked his head and listened to the thunderous bellowing. The noise was blood-curdling, and yet there was a strangely piteous quality to it. Listening intently, the man walked cautiously toward where he knew the trapped bear must be waiting. His little dog, Jenny, which had been sleeping next to him, was cringing against his legs, making it difficult to walk. Suddenly, the bear fell silent. Clark continued to move ahead in the darkness, straining his ears, peering into the dark, searching for any telltale movement that might divulge the bear's presence.

His blood ran cold when the roaring began again— this time from behind him. With no moon to light the way, he must have passed the grizzly somewhere along the trail. Clark was no coward, but neither was he a fool. He knew Old Ephraim would make short shrift of him if he found him alone in the dark. Clark looked around. He scrambled up the hillside and climbed into the first substantial tree he reached. Then he waited for Ephraim to make the next move. Jenny cowered at the base of Clark's tree. Then Clark made a dreadful discovery: He'd forgotten to put on his pants when he'd left camp. And his extra ammunition was still inside his pants pockets.

Clark's seven-shot .25-35 rifle was a dependable firearm, but hardly what you might term a grizzly gun. Grizzlies, as he knew, usually took a lot of killing. And now here he sat, treed like a coon, with just seven shells to finish off perhaps the most infamous grizzly of all time. Clark thought about this until dawn. Then he shinnied back down the tree and thought a moment more.

Everything was quiet; too quiet, to Clark's way of thinking. Somewhere out there lurked the great bear. Clark couldn't help but wonder what the bear had in mind, for Old Ephraim was not the type to take such an insult lying down. The man decided not to take the main trail back to his campsite. Instead, he'd slip along the other side of the draw. He'd moved quite a distance when he heard the bear roar once again.

Clark stopped. The bear was close, very close. He cocked his gun and made his decision. He would seek out Old Ephraim.

The roaring came from a patch of willows directly in the man's path. Clark traveled boldly until he finally could make out what appeared to be a grizzled gray shape hunched over in the willows. When he discerned what seemed to be movement not ten yards away, Clark took hasty aim and fired. The bullet screamed through the early morning silence, and, at the same instant, a huge, shaggy beast reared high above the man's head.

At that moment Clark questioned his common sense. The bear was immense and, as Clark later said, it looked at least fifteen feet high. The bear hovered over the man, twisting slowly, trying to use its fabulous sense of smell to sniff out the enemy. Clark did the only thing he could do. He froze. One false move, and at this distance it would be all over.

As the man stared at Old Ephraim, the reason for the animal's painful outburst of the previous night became clear. A steel trap hung from the bear's left forepaw. Jagged steel teeth had sliced deep into its flesh. The chain, which had wrapped itself several times around the bear's leg, added even more misery. The bear had a noble demeanor despite the blood that frothed from its mouth. Desperate to free himself, Old Ephraim had spent the night champing and chewing at the despicable contraption that had entrapped him at the wallow.

Finally, the grizzly noticed Clark. Something clicked in the beast's head, almost as though he recognized the silent man as the source of all his troubles. Old Ephraim made up his mind. He charged, bulling his way through the tangle of willows and alders. Clark could barely stand upright in his boots, but he knew he must make his next shot count. He steadied himself and pulled the trigger.

The bear dropped to the ground, bloody foam spewing from his muzzle. Then he lurched back up and continued onward, determined to reach Clark. Again and again Clark fired. But nothing seemed to stop the grizzly. Six times Clark shot. Six times the bear fell. And six times the bear surged to his feet and narrowed the distance between himself and the man.

When Old Ephraim was less than two yards away, Clark bolted. He raced as quickly as he could through the scrub brush, Old Ephraim fast on his heels. The only thing that was saving the man from the grizzly's implacable jaws was the painful steel trap with its long, heavy chain and log drag, which hindered the animal's every movement. Clark didn't dare look back. To risk even a glance was to court disaster. He wished at this moment that he'd never even heard of Old Ephraim.

At that moment the man became aware of yet another sound: the yapping of Jenny. Concerned for his pet, Clark looked behind him. He saw Old Ephraim only ten yards away and the little dog biting and yapping at the bear. Clark could hardly believe his eyes as he watched the terrier worry the larger animal, nipping at its hind legs and distracting the brute from the fleeing man. Clark saw his chance. He leaned against a tree to steady his rifle and, with his last shell, took Old

Ephraim's life. When his legs stopped shaking, Clark walked up to his fallen adversary. His final bullet had entered the bear's brain from behind its ear.

When Sam Kemp returned to the scene, he found an incredulous Clark. The two men examined Old Ephraim's carcass and discovered he measured 9 feet, 11 inches from nose to tail. Two of Clark's bullets had actually pierced the old monarch's heart yet hadn't been enough to stop him. Only the final shot, the one that had penetrated the animal's brain, had been enough to do the job.

Kemp and Clark buried what was left of the bear because their horses were much too skittish to be packed with either head or hide.

Clark never boasted of his exploit. Whether it was because he was so grateful to be alive or because he realized that he had single-handedly destroyed one of the frontier's last legends, no one can say. But at least once each summer, for the rest of his life, Clark would ride to visit Old Ephraim's grave. Clark knew exactly where he'd buried the grand old beast. He'd made the marker himself. It read, "Here lies Old Ephraim. He gave Frank Clark a good scare."

21

Grizzlies with a Taste for Man

Grizzlies, like humans, can acquire tastes. But no acquired taste is as deadly as the one a grizzly develops for human flesh. Thankfully, such a thing rarely occurs. Yet it does happen. Perhaps the most famous example took place in the late 1800s in western Canada. Andy Russell, writing in *Grizzly Country*, reproduced a letter written over sixty years ago to Colonel Townsend Whelen by F.H. "Bert" Riggall that describes just such a grisly occurrence.

❖ ❖ ❖

When Stewart Edward White wrote of "Dangerous Game" in the *Saturday Evening Post*, he never mentioned "Grizzlies and Small-pox," but when you interpose the word "Indian" between, it tells a whole lot that is generally not known about bears. Forty to sixty years ago the Indians here (Stonies) camped in small groups all through the mountains in the sheep, deer, goat, and bear country, and while so camped, in would ride a relative from a smallpox infested camp, and in ten days half the camp would be dead or dying, and the survivors would leave all the teepees standing and ride off to spread the plague to other camps. Pretty soon the grizzlies here found that they could invade the teepees without fear and feed on the dead, and after a while on the dying, and from that it was only a step, soon taken, to hunting the unaffected Indians in after years, and they did so hunt them in certain sections, and taught their cubs to do so also; and some of these cubs are alive today, the Stonies declare, and I believe them! When I came here this was wonderful hunting country (inside the mountains), simply because the Stonies were too afraid of these grizzlies to venture into the game country, and up the best canyons no old Indian trails led through the timber at the mouths to the basins at the heads. I had to cut these trails myself; and although each spring and fall bands of Stonies passed, none would venture over my trails, and some of them at different times told me why, and warned me that the bears there were bad actors and would smell and stalk an Indian, and myself also if I did not watch out! I had two *very* close calls from bears there the first year or two, and killed both bears within a few feet of me, and I believe that these bears were old timers who knew what human flesh tasted like and were not averse to trying it again. I have since shot and killed grizzlies in many places as far north as the Big Smokey and down in Montana on both sides of the Divide, and I know that without question the bears here and just across the British Columbia and Montana are more savage and aggressive than in other sections. I am sure that this is not generally appreciated or known, so I have gone into some detail, as I think you will find it interesting and probably new.

PART

Early Black Bear Attacks

III

22

The Myth of the Black Bear

Along the eastern seaboard and westward to the middle of the continent, the black bear peacefully shared the forests with Native Americans. These people, well versed in the ways of the natural world, had come to revere the black bear as a wise and honored guest.

In the world of the revolving sky, the Great Bear, *Ursa Major*, was the symbol of renewal and of rebirth. When the people looked upward, they watched the bear being chased around the North Star by hunters, or in some cultures by birds of prey. In mid-autumn, the chase would end when the bear was caught. The hunters then ate the bear's flesh and left his skeleton lying on its back close to the winter horizon. In spring, the people would rejoice, for once more the bear was resurrected.

The Algonquin people believed the bear could cure their ills. The grandfather of all had vast, untapped powers. If game was scarce, the bear could deliver it. Many of their holiest ceremonies were modeled after the great mystery of bear hibernation, including puberty rites, shaman ceremonies, purification rites, and initiations into secret ceremonies. All followed a common pattern: isolation, fasting, symbolic death, and rebirth.

Initiates would first be separated from their families and villages. They would be taken to a secluded hut or cave, or perhaps simply lie hidden beneath a blanket, hidden from the outward world much as a bear is during its winter sleep. While isolated, they would neither drink nor eat. Sometimes they were tortured to test their fortitude. The rite would also include a visit from a tribal elder who would divulge to them the tribe's secrets or the secrets of the society they were about to enter. Symbolically, the person who once had been was dead. When the novice emerged from isolation as a new person, it was an act of rebirth directly paralleling the bear's reemergence in the spring.

Menstruating women were also isolated during the time of their periods. By far the most dangerous time to be around a young woman, these Indians believed, was during her first menses. Although it now seems politically incorrect to even describe such ancient beliefs, an Ojibwa girl about to start her first period was called *wemukowe*, which means "going to be a bear." During her isolation she would be called *mukowe*, or "she is a bear." Her people believed that her powers during this time were so great that if she glanced at or touched someone it could bring them paralysis, or death, or cause destruction of the berry crop.

Sweat lodges used by Indians to purify their bodies were constructed to resemble grandfather bear. Bent branches resembling a bear's ribs formed the shell, and the entire structure was then covered with bearskin.

Because of their importance and relative abundance, black bears were a popular subject for North American myth making, be it by Native Americans, white settlers, or black slaves. Here is one legend of the Creeks and Cherokees, recounted in *Native American Myths and*

Legends, which tells of a time when their people were almost destroyed by famine.

> After repeated treks into the forests in search of food, the elders called a great meeting. "This may be the end of us," they said, "for we can find nothing to eat." At the time of this great meeting, there were eight clans among our People. The members of the eighth clan decided upon a solution. They visited the elders and said, "We have decided to die so that our brothers may live." And then they walked into the forest.
>
> Several days later, they returned with such a great growth of black hair all over their bodies that the villagers did not even recognize them. But since they offered themselves, their starving kinsmen shot them and ate them.
>
> One hunter who came upon a family of bears was reluctant to kill them. "But you are my brothers," he said. "It is meant that you should kill us," they told him. "Our flesh will nourish you, and our souls will not die but will return to the Spirit World to be clothed once more with flesh so that we may visit you again." And that is why hunters must kneel by the slain bear and say, "Thank you, my brother."

The Cree Indians of what is now Ontario and northeastern Manitoba believed that respect shown to the animals was of paramount importance in determining the tribe's fortunes. If hunters honored the animals they killed, the animals' spirit keepers, or *Memekwesiw*, the spirit boss, would be pleased and release even more animals that could, once free, choose to offer themselves for killing. Bear hunts, which involved the most powerful spirit keeper, had to follow the strictest rituals of all.

The traditional Cree bear hunt involved two separate phases. Bear hunts took place in early spring when Cree food supplies were at their lowest ebb. Since only denned bears were to be hunted, the bear hunt had a better chance of success than did a hunt for caribou or for moose.

The Cree, like most Native Americans, relied on dreams to give them direction. They felt that while they dreamed, the spirit boss of the bears would reveal where a bear might be found. "This is where you will find him," the spirit boss would say. *Memekwesiw* would also divulge to the hunter his own special song for the impending hunt.

The hunter would venture into the woods to the place decreed by *Memekwesiw* and look for the denning bear's air hole, which, ideally, would be ringed with yellowish-brown frost proving the bear was still inside.

With a den located, the hunter returned home. He sang his bear hunt song, accompanying himself with drum or rattle, possibly repeating words such as "He knows I am coming." He would now place himself in a trance, and the entire hunt would become vivid in his dreamlike state.

He would then take a sweat bath to cleanse his body. He would wear his finest clothing to please the bear. Any new gear could not be used unless it had first been purified by being placed on a newly killed bear carcass for a time. The hunter would initiate his newest gear once this bear had been killed.

A hunter who was "for bear" was not allowed to change his mind were he to come across easier game. That would be unfaithful to the bear. *Memekwesiw* would know, and he would be displeased.

When the hunter reached the bear's den, he waited outside, calling, "Grandfather! It is warm! Time to come out!" If the bear did not emerge, he would call it "grandmother." The Cree believed the bear would be angry unless it was called by a special name.

When the bear left its den, the Cree prescribed that it be killed with ax, spear, or club so that hunter and bear were more evenly matched. Bows and guns would not be nearly powerful enough for the bear's spirit. With ax, spear, or club, the hunter would get close to the bear. He would feel the animal's death, and would reach in to touch its spirit. His goal was to kill it with one sharp blow, although this was rarely achieved.

Afterward, the bear's carcass was placed on its back. Tobacco was arranged upon its chest. The hunter would sit next to the bear and say, "Do not be angry. I killed you because I am hungry. I need your skin for my coat, your meat so my family can eat. We have nothing to eat. See how fine you look now? It is good to be killed by me. Return to *Memekwesiw*. Tell him how well I have treated you."

The way the hunter treated the bear's carcass, the way he conducted himself back in camp, and the way in which the bear was served to tribesmen were all dictated by a set of rigid guidelines. A hunter who boasted about killing such an animal dishonored himself and his people. The bear had made a gift of its life. For a hunter to take credit for such a wondrous gift violated his pact with the bear's spirit and with *Memekwesiw*.

The black bear of North American myth and legend also contributed to the aura surrounding Davy Crockett, the famous American folk hero. Crockett was already an accomplished bear hunter by the time he served in the Creek Wars between 1813 and 1815.

According to Paul Schullery, writing in *The Bear Hunter's Century*, only one authentic contemporary work was based on actual events that took place during Crockett's life. This was *A Narrative of the Life of David Crockett of the State of Tennessee*, written by Crockett himself in collaboration with Thomas Chilton, a Kentucky congressman. In this book Crockett said, "Of all the hunting I ever did, I have always delighted most in bear hunting."

Crockett, like most men of the frontier, seemed to have taken to heart some of the Native Americans' spiritual beliefs. One day he told two companions heading out after turkeys that, "I was for larger game." He went on to explain in *A Narrative of the Life of David Crockett of the State of Tennessee*, excerpted by Paul Schullery in *The Bear Hunter's Century*:

> ". . . [I] dreamed the night before of having a hard fight with a big black nigger, and I knowed it was a sign that I was to have a battle with a bear; for in bear country, I never know'd such a dream to fail."

Though today's reader may take umbrage at what appears to be a totally insensitive statement, people of the early eighteenth century did not regard the word "nigger" as having racial overtones. It was a favorite word of frontiersmen and mountain men who used it freely to jokingly describe one another. According to many biographers of the day—and even today's *The American Heritage Dictionary*—the term originally meant only an "ignorant person," and was not an insult aimed specifically at black people.

In 1845, Abraham Lincoln, whom many modern animal rightists embrace as one of the first Americans having empathy for animals, penned a poem entitled, *The Bear Hunt*. Because he was acquainted with so many different details, it is probable that Lincoln, during his early life, participated in many such events. Here is Lincoln's little-known work, which should hold an honored place in any mythology of the black bear:

❖ ❖ ❖

The Bear Hunt

A wild bear chase didst never see?
Then has thou lived in vain—
Thy richest bump of glorious glee
Lies desert in thy brain.
When first my father settled here,

191

'Twas then the frontier line;
The panther's scream filled night with fear
And bears preyed on the swine.

But woe for bruin's short-lived fun
When rose the squealing cry;
Now man and horse, with dog and gun
For vengeance at him fly.

A sound of danger strikes his ear;
He gives the breeze a snuff;
Away he bounds, with little fear,
And seeks the tangled rough.

On press his foes, and reach the ground
Where's left his half-munched meal;
The dogs, in circles, scent around
And find his fresh made trail.

With instant cry, away they dash,
And men as fast pursue;
O'er logs they leap, through water splash
And shout the brisk halloo.

Now to elude the eager pack
Bear shuns the open ground,
Through matted vines he shapes his track,
And runs it, round and round.

The tall, fleet cur, with deep-mouthed voice
Now speeds him, as the wind;
While half-grown pup, and short-legged fice
Are yelping far behind.

And fresh recruits are dropping in
To join the merry corps;
With yelp and yell, a mingled din—
The woods are in a roar—

And round, and round the chase now goes,
The world's alive with fun;
Nick Carter's horse his rider throws,
And Mose Hills drops his gun.

Now, sorely pressed, bear glances back,
And lolls his tired tongue,
When as, to force him from his track
An ambush on him sprung.

Across the glade he sweeps for flight,
And fully is in view—
The dogs, new fired by the sight
Their cry and speed renew.

The foremost ones now reach his rear;
He turns, they dash away,
And circling now the wrathful bear
They have him full at bay.

At top of speed the horsemen come,
All screaming in a row—
'Whoop!' 'Take him, Tiger!' 'Seize him, Drum!'
Bang—bang! the rifles go!

And furious now, the dogs he tears,
And crushes in his ire—
Wheels right and left, and upward rears,
With eyes of burning fire.

But leaden death is at his heart—
Vain all the strength he plies,
And, spouting blood from every part,
He reels, and sinks, and dies!

And now a dinsome clamor rose,—
'But who should have his skin?'
Who first draws blood, each hunter knows
This prize must always win.

But, who did this, and how to trace
What's true from what's a lie,—
Like lawyers in a murder case
They stoutly argufy.

Aforesaid fice, of blustering mood,
Behind, and quite forgot,
Just now emerging from the wood
Arrives upon the spot.

With grinning teeth, and up-turned hair
Brim full of spunk and wrath,
He growls, and seizes on dead bear
And shakes for life and death—

And swells, as if his skin would tear,
And growls, and shakes again,
And swears, as plain as dog can swear
That he has won the skin!

Conceited whelp! we laugh at thee,
Nor mind that not a few
Of pompous, two legged dogs there be
Conceited quite as you.

The black bear has also been celebrated in the tales of Uncle Remus, written during the late nineteenth century by author Joel Chandler Harris. Beloved by children and adults alike, Harris's fables generated a great deal of interest in American wildlife. His main characters, B'rer Fox, B'rer Rabbit, and B'rer Bear, were continually in trouble. While Harris depicted both fox and rabbit as cunning and wily, B'rer Bear was illustrated as being strong and mighty, but a touch dimwitted, far from the way most modern biologists view this amazing animal.

And far from the way one of our most renowned writers viewed it as well. Here is an excerpt from William Faulkner's novella, *The Bear*, in which he puts into incomparable words the special feeling evoked in those who love bears:

> He realized later that it had begun long before that. It had already begun on that day when he first wrote his age in two ciphers and his cousin McCaslin brought him for the first time to the camp, the big woods, to earn for himself from the wilderness the name and state of hunter provided he in his turn were humble and enduring enough. He had already inherited then, without ever having seen it, the big old bear with one trap-ruined foot that in an area almost a hundred miles square had earned for himself a name, a definite designation like a living man:—the long legend of corncribs pulled down and rifled, of shoats and grown pigs and even calves carried bodily into the woods and devoured and traps and deadfalls overthrown and dogs mangled and slain and shotgun and even rifle shots delivered at point-blank range yet with no more effect than so many peas blown through a tube by a child— a corridor of wreckage and destruction beginning back before the boy was born, through which sped, not fast but rather with the ruthless and irresistible deliberation of a locomotive, the shaggy tremendous, red-eyed, not malevolent but just big, too big for the dogs which tried to bay it, for the horses which tried to ride it down, for the men and the bullets they fired into it; too big for the very country which was its constricting scope. It was as if the boy had already divined what his senses and intellect had not encompassed yet; that doomed wilderness whose edges were being constantly and punily gnawed at by men with plows and axes who feared it because it was wilderness, men myriad and nameless even to one another in the land where the old bear had earned a name, and through which ran not even a mortal beast but an anachronism indomitable and invincible out of an old dead time, a phantom, epitome and apotheosis of the old wild life which the little puny humans swarmed and hacked at in a fury of abhorrence and fear like pygmies about the ankles of a drowsing elephant;—the old bear, solitary,

indomitable, and alone; widowered childless and absolved of mortality—old Priam reft of his old wife and outlived all his sons.

23

The Fate of Frances Downey

On the vast American frontier of the late eighteenth century, the black bear quickly became the subject of lore and legend. The Americans embellished each tale of the bear's might until it was well suited to be shared around various campfires. The frontiersmen had learned respect for the bear not only from the great animal itself, but from the Native Americans who regarded bears with something akin to awe.

Some tribes would stage elaborate hunts for these great beasts, which often weighed 500 pounds or more. Tribal leaders would send a line of as many as 500 warriors through the timber to drive out bears to open ground. Lying in wait would be another phalanx of warriors armed with spears, and when the bear charged into the open, the waiting warriors would be ready for it.

Youths such as Kentucky's Frances Downey were well acquainted with such tales. And they knew as well how frontiersmen as rugged as Davy Crockett had built the foundations of their own rapidly accumulating legend around the ubiquitous black bear. White hunters were more proficient at taking these creatures than the Indians because they had the advantages of rifles and steel traps; still, any hunter who could kill forty-seven black bears in a single month, as Davy Crockett was supposed to have done, was quite a hunter indeed.

Bears were probably the last thing on Frances Downey's mind that long-ago summer of 1787. He and a friend were searching for one of Downey's stray horses when three Indians suddenly sprang on them from ambush. Downey's companion had just enough time to raise his rifle and fire. Fortunately, the shot was true; one of the Indians fell dead to the ground.

Startled and enraged, the two remaining Indians took off after the Kentuckians. One chased Downey; the other began running after Downey's friend (whose name is lost to history). Downey's companion stopped, abruptly turned, and stabbed at the warrior with his knife, wounding him badly. With the Indian hurt, Downey's friend made good his escape.

Young Downey seemed doomed. His pursuer was gaining on him rapidly, tomahawk in hand and evil intentions clearly evident. Downey's only hope lay in finding a place to hide. He dashed around a large tree and threw himself into a patch of thick underbrush, the Indian fast on his heels.

One of the frontier's early reporters takes up the account: "It so happened—was it Providence?—that a large she-bear had made her bed underneath the roots where the ferocious beast was then suckling her cubs.

"As the astonished savage arose to his feet, the furious bear sprang upon him, and with a terrible hug, grasped him in her powerful arms, the Indian giving an unearthly yell from the great pain." While the Indian battled for his life, Downey escaped.

The next day, the two settlers returned to the scene. They found the she-bear lying dead, but they could find no sign of the Indian. No one ever knew whether the match had been a draw—if the bear had also slain the Indian and his tribe had borne away his body. Perhaps—against all odds—the Indian was able to use some desperate maneuver to escape the jaws and claws of the furious animal.

24

Hand to Paw
with a Black Bear:
Wade Hampton

Wade Hampton III was one of the South's most decorated Civil War heroes. He left the service of the Confederacy with the rank of general of the cavalry, was a famous hunter and horseman, and owned several vast holdings, including one in South Carolina called "The Woodlands." He inherited this latter piece of property from his father, a Revolutionary War hero, and owned yet another estate in Washington County, Mississippi, which had been purchased solely as a hunting preserve and was called "Bear Garden." General Hampton served not only as South Carolina's governor but as its U.S. Senator during the years 1878-1890.

Hampton hunted bears in the manner of most Southern gentlemen of the day: galloping behind a pack of baying hounds. Recognized all over the world as perhaps the finest horseman of the epoch, Hampton was also widely acknowledged to be the bravest of bear hunters, often killing the beasts with a hand-held knife wielded at close quarters. Theodore Roosevelt believed Hampton had "been in at the death of" 500 bears, "at least two-thirds of them falling by his own hand."

In *The Wilderness Hunter*, Roosevelt reported that Hampton had killed "thirty or forty" bears with the knife and was hurt only once when he was "rather severely torn in the forearm."

Readers interested in historic bear attacks—even ones that were more or less provoked—owe a debt of gratitude to Paul Schullery, who, in researching *The Bear Hunter's Century*, unearthed this account from the early sporting magazine, *Turf, Field and Farm* entitled "My Bear Hunt with Gen. Wade Hampton." This article was written by "Greybeard," the pen name taken by one of General Hampton's companions on what may have been one of this Southern bear-hunting legend's most thrilling outings.

> "Now," said the Colonel [Hampton], "if you are not familiar with the bear, be careful. Don't take him into close quarters. Put a ball through his heart before he can reach you with his paws; but if you fail to do this, stand not on the order of your going— leave! And, by the way," he added, "whatever you do, save the dogs."

I knew as much about bear hunting as I did about elephants; had seen the beast tame in menageries, and once or twice encountered a live one, but no rifle shot of mine had ever yet penetrated the shaggy coat of a bruin, and my ambition was on edge to be gratified. Besides, I had just come from "the Plains," and felt big with the reputation which all fledglings innately enjoy who have knocked down a dozen or twenty buffalo. Well, we separated and got to work, I taking the stand which the colonel had assigned to me, to await his movements and those of the dogs, who were to drive up the game while he made a circuit. Whither he went or what he did, I have no knowledge. I only remember that for nearly two hours I waited patiently, listening to every sound, trembling with expectation, and brave down to the pulp of my index finger that rested on the trigger of my trusty rifle. In fact, I had begun to grow dreamy, and thoughts were wandering among the scenes of home life far eastward. Suddenly, there was a long halloo—a shot, and then another. The dogs were baying, and evidently in full pursuit of game. What it was, whether of deer or bear, of course, I had no means of knowing; but instinctively I felt that it was coming toward the little branch whereon I had been stationed. It was a question of less than five minutes, but in that interval I enjoyed the keen zest of a sportsman's expectation. I had it settled in my mind where I was to send my rifle-ball, where I would bleed my trophy when down, and what I would do in various triumphant contingencies that were pictured in my mind. But, alas! the schemes of men "aft gang agley." Bruin—for it was a full-sized beast of that nomenclature—made his appearance with a rush, tearing through the cane-brake, a hound hanging to one ear, and the pack close on his heels. I raised my rifle and fired, and have long been satisfied that the bullet sped at least fifteen feet above its mark. At any rate, it didn't hit him, while the sound of the discharge served to draw his attention to a new and unexpected adversary, and that was your humble servant. Despite the fact that he carried the weight of a dog and a bullet from the gun of Gen. Hampton, he turned his blood-red eyes on me, and with an ugly expression around his mouth, which I regarded at the time as physiognomically dangerous, made directly for the position I occupied. At the same instant, a brace of hounds, God bless 'em! dashing through the cane with a glad yelp and a bound, seized the bear, one by the haunches and another by the flank. The digression saved me. I had no other resource than to take to a tree or the bush. I never was good at climbing, and chose the latter, plunging pell-mell into the cane, with an impetus like unto that of a demoralized locomotive. Fortunately, I struck a path—one of those narrow openings which are sometimes worn on the Mississippi bottoms by animals making their way to water. But, horror of horrors! I had not proceeded fifty yards before I heard close behind the sound of the pursuing bear. Frantic with the pain of the chawing bites every instant penetrating his flesh, and unable to shake off the faithful dogs, Bruin had doubtless taken one of his old routes, and instinctively hoped to brush or shake his tormentors off in the thick undergrowth. On he came—closer and closer—the brittle reeds crackling under his feet; the hounds giving their short, sharp, ugly yelps, and I dashing forward as best I could through the almost impenetrable mass. It seemed as if I could feel the hot breath of the brute upon my back, and I realized, as only a man in such an emergency can do, that if once he laid his claws upon me, I was a dead man. My knife was already drawn. Life seemed to hang but by a thread, and I was prepared to do battle over that thin tie while there was a muscle left to put forth its strength.

Yet stay! Suddenly—in less time than I can describe it—there was a crashing of reeds in front of me. In an instant more, Gen. Hampton, hot and flushed with pursuit, his clothes torn, and his fine face lighted up with that keen, bold expression which I can fancy illuminated it on many another occasion in the hour of danger afterwards, stood face to face with me. It was but a second. He took in the situation at a glance. Like myself, he could almost feel the presence of the bear now twenty steps behind. Seizing me by the breast, he pushed me back into the wilderness of canes perhaps three or four feet—at any rate, out of the narrow path—and exclaimed, as I fell backward, "Stay there, as you value your life. Don't move an inch!" At the same moment, darting forward, he dropped on his knee, and, cocking his rifle, waited. I can't describe the interval, it was so short; but it seemed as if before I could gasp, the bear was on him. He fired, coolly and steadily as if he were shooting at ducks. The bear gave a groan, but the pace was unslacked. He dashed on, up to the very muzzle of the remaining gun barrel. The general was in the act of pulling the trigger, when a cane, slipping from under his feet, flew upward, like a spring, and striking the weapon, the gun was discharged high in the air. In the twinkling of an eye, the general was on the ground, struck down by the forepaw of the enraged brute, but knife in hand, and as cool as if promenading his own piazza. I sprang forward to his assistance, but he shouted to me to stand back. He was lying almost at full length with the bear, while the latter was being torn and distracted by the dogs, now in full force, and doubly frantic, seeing their master in his power. It was but the work of a moment, but I shouldn't forget the scene in a month of centuries. The general's right arm and knife were under the animal, but with a motion as quick as a flash, he threw the other arm over the body, and clutching the knife, drove it deep into the heart of the brute. There was a spasmodic stroke of the paw in the direction of the stroke of the blade, for a bear always strikes out in the direction from which it experiences pain—a fact, by the way, which saved the face and body of the general—and after a short convulsive spasm, the monster lay dead. And that is all. The dogs, with their jaws all bloody, were called off, save one, who lay in the brake panting its death agony from wounds it had received. The general recovered [to] his feet without a scratch; gathered his gun, wiped the bloody knife in the dark fur; sheathed it in an every day sort of fashion; the Negroes came up, and after extravagantly pouring forth their congratulations with true Ethiopian enthusiasm, secured the carcass, and the whole party reunited around the camp fire at night fall, well satisfied with the adventures of the day.

Early Polar Bear Attacks

25

The Myth
of the Polar Bear

Indigenous Arctic peoples held many of the same beliefs as the Native Americans who inhabited the continent's more southerly regions. This is hardly surprising since the common ancestors of all indigenous American peoples made the same great journey across the ancient Beringia isthmus. These early wanderers were unaware that they had just entered a land devoid of humans. To find better hunting, they simply started traveling east. Some people stayed in the northlands; others continued on south, searching—as do people of today—for a better life.

That life consisted of hunting and gathering, and was eventually to include commerce between many far-flung tribes. But similarities between the people persisted. Like others of their race, Arctic people believed animals possessed souls. This belief was so fundamental, it permeated every aspect of their daily lives. People of the Arctic also believed animals would occasionally "cross over" the barrier between themselves and humans. One myth of the Greenland Eskimos as related in *Northern Tales: Traditional Stories of Eskimo & Indian Peoples,* goes like this:

The Bear Goes on His Solitary Journey

As sometimes happened between the People and the animals, a young male polar bear fell in love with a beautiful Eskimo woman, Tipi, who was already married to Inuk, a great hunter. While Inuk was gone, Nanuq—Nanook—would snuggle up against the woman within her warm igloo. Nanuq did not care, for Inuk was out hunting bear. And anyway, Nanuq loved Tipi.

Nanuq told Tipi, "I would love to have a little wife like you." And he told her where he lived so that one day, if she should change her mind and grow tired of Inuk, she could come to him. "But," he warned, growing fearful, "don't ever tell Inuk where I live. No matter where I may be, I will hear you."

"Ieh . . . ieh," little Tipi answered, moving even closer to her lover, Nanuq.

Inuk, although a great hunter, was having bad luck finding bear. As the days passed, his humor worsened. He would enter their igloo, sniff the air and say, "Tipi! It smells so bad in here, almost like a bear had been here."

But his wife denied it. She denied it until Inuk became so unhappy she could no longer stand it. "I care for nothing," Inuk finally said, "except killing a bear."

One night, when once again he had pushed Tipi away, she leaned close to his ear and whispered, "Nanuq."

"Where?" Inuk cried, leaping for his harpoon. And she told him, betraying Nanuq, her lover.

The man ran from the igloo. He flew up the mountain with his harpoon and dogs. But when he reached the bear's den, it was empty. Nanuq had heard.

Back home, Tipi hid within the igloo. She trembled badly, for she knew what she had done. She heard a rumbling like thunder within the mountain, and she was full of fear.

It was Nanuq. Panting hard, he ran down and ran straight to the igloo. He stood high upon his back legs and reached up with his paw, as though to crush it to the ice. But then he stopped.

Betrayed and sorrowful beyond all words, Nanuq began his long, solitary journey, a journey that continues today.

Since animals died so that humans might live, it was vital for hunters to maintain a harmonious relationship with the hunted. Failure to follow sacred rituals once a kill had been made might cause game such as polar bears to desert the area. When a human died, Arctic peoples would cease work for several days as a sign of respect. When Nanook—the great white bear—died, they did the same.

Knud Rasmussen, who journeyed from Greenland to Alaska's western coast on the Fifth Thule Expedition, made friends with several Arctic shamans who told him of their daily struggles. William Mills, writing in *Bears and Men: A Gathering*, describes what they said:

> Aua, of the Iglulik Eskimo on Hudson Bay, explained to Rasmussen the special relation that hunting people had with the forces of their world, and how such forces were inescapable. "We fear the souls of dead human beings and of the animals we have killed." And his brother added, "The greatest peril of life lies in the fact that human food consists entirely of souls." There, in the succinctest of statements, is the world of the hunter illuminated.

Of all the animal spirits, the bear's was considered the most powerful and, potentially, the most dangerous. Native people believed that once a bear had been killed, its soul remained on the tip of the hunter's spear for four or five days. If certain rituals were not followed, the bear's spirit could easily become menacing, and that would bode ill for the people of the village. To ward off potential evil from the bear's spirit, such as a possible attack, all work would cease for a set number of days. The bear's skin had to be displayed outside the dwelling place of the hunter and surrounded with tools—women's tools for a female bear; men's for a male. Gifts and offerings to the bear's soul were laid upon the skin.

These people further believed that a polar bear's soul, or *innua*, resided in its bladder. When a bear had been killed by the Inuit, the people of the eastern Canadian Arctic, its bladder would be removed, inflated, dried, and then perhaps decorated and hung indoors. A bladder feast would be held to honor the dead bear. If proper respect were not given, the *innua* might turn into a monster.

When the Inuit chase Nanook with their sledges, they bound after him in a state of high excitement, yelling "Nanook!" As the men draw near, they release their sled dogs. The dogs rush the white bear, snapping and snarling; however, Nanook does not wait idly by. He pops and snaps his jaws and will disable or kill as many dogs as he can. Finally, the hunters kill Nanook with rifles or spears. The bear falls down, never again to rise. The hunters then position his body with his head pointing toward their village so that Nanook's spirit knows which way to carry home the tale of the successful hunt. Before the carcass is skinned, the bear's head must be repositioned to face east, the direction from which the spirit keeper will either dispatch the soul of this bear or another to take its place.

Nanook was always an integral part of Arctic life. When Rasmussen asked an elderly Inuit to define life's greatest happiness, the old man replied, "To run across fresh bear tracks and be ahead of everyone else." Those who treasure bears and the last remaining wilderness would have to agree.

26

Early Polar
Bear Attacks

All explorers are, by necessity, people of adventurous spirit. Early adventurers who ultimately conquered the Far North were deterred by nothing: not ice, nor cold, nor even the prospect of becoming ice-bound for months when their ships became trapped and useless within the rapidly freezing sea.

Always on the lookout for treasure to carry back to their homes, as well as for exciting tales to relate to their shipmates and loved ones, the first European explor-ers of the northern seas were probably as apt to engage giant bears in combat as the mountain men of the Rockies would be more than two centuries later. For unless these men were engaged in active exploration, they had plenty of time on their hands. Any chance to test their mettle proved a welcome diversion. What better way to do so than by giving chase to the great white bear of the North, whose hide was thick and warm and whose meat could be eaten in an emergency?

People who inhabited those portions of Europe and Asia above the Arctic Circle had been familiar with white bears for years. But the first account by a white man of polar bears on the North American continent may have been this one, recorded in 1585 by John Davis. Davis had just sailed into Cumberland Sound on the southeast coast of Baffin Island when he observed the following:

> . . . So soone as we were come to an anker in Totnes rode under mount Raleigh we espied four white beares at the foote of the mount. We, supposing them to bee goates or wolves, manned our boats, and went toward them: but when wee came neere the shore, we found them to be white beares of a monstrous bignesse.

The Barents Sea is named for Dutch explorer Willem Barents. On 19 August 1595, Barents arrived at the narrow strait between Novaya Zemlya and Siberia, the gateway to the Kara Sea. He wanted to proceed, but the channel was shut down by ice floes that ground and crushed against each other, producing an alarming amount of noise. Stalled for the time being, Barents's crew was sent ashore on nearby Staten Island to hunt Arctic hares. After several hours of activity, two of the sailors decided to take their rest. The men lay down on their stomachs for a short while when one of them felt something cold grip him about the throat. Gerrit De Veer, Barents's chronicler, recorded the exchange:

"Who is it that pulls me so by the neck?" he asked.

"Oh, mate, it is a bear!"

So gasped his companion, who promptly ran for help. But by the time twenty armed men arrived, it was already too late for the unlucky sailor who had been set upon by the bear. De Veer continued with his tale:

. . . The cruel, fierce, and ravenous beast had fallen upon the man, bit his head in sunder, and sucked out his blood.

The bear, a lean female, was still beside her prey as the men approached. The men rose up as one body and charged the beast, using every weapon at their disposal. They shot muskets, wielded them as clubs, and stabbed with their pikes. But this polar bear was a fighter. She seized yet another sailor and devoured him as his companions watched in horror. Finally, someone managed to shoot the animal between the eyes while the rest of the men slashed it with their cutlasses. But the bear wasn't done yet. De Veer wrote that she held the man still fast by the neck, and lifted up her head with the man in her mouth.

The pilot, a brave man, dared to rush the animal. He smashed his musket hard against the bear's snout, and she fell to the ground with a deafening roar. The pilot wasted no time. He slit the bear's throat with his knife, and her blood poured out on the frozen ground. The men then buried their dead comrades. When they returned to their ship, they carried with them the bearskin that had been paid for with the blood of their companions.

De Veer's meticulous accounts later detail another fierce battle between Barents's crew and a polar bear. This time, the sailors were scouting one of the Arctic's many islands when they caught sight of a swimming polar bear that De Veer describes as "twelve feet tall." They gave chase and battled the huge animal for four hours, using "muskets, halberds, and hatchets." But the bear would not yield her spirit. She refused to surrender until finally "we cut her head in sunder with an ax." This adventure made such an impression on the crew that Barents decided to dub the island his men had been scouting "Bear Island," a name it still holds today.

In the late nineteenth century, two Arctic natives decided to go hunting for food. They were hoping to find a seal or two, and since it was wintertime, they knew that their chances of success would increase were they to separate. According to the tale, one of the men somehow lost his spear. He was alone on the ice, unsure of where to find his companion, when he realized he was being stalked by Nanook. At first he froze in his tracks. Then as the mighty bear slowly came closer, the man collapsed upon the ice. He lay there completely still, willing his body to cease even the slightest movement. He held his breath, fearful that if his chest heaved, Nanook might pounce and, with one blow of his paw, send him to meet his ancestors.

Nanook was plainly curious about the unmoving lump that lay seal-like upon the ice. The great bear moved closer and closer. At last the animal pressed its black nose right against the native's face. But the man didn't move. He didn't dare.

Nanook was clearly reluctant to leave what might be a meal upon the ice. It sniffed the man everywhere and pushed against his fur-clad body, but the man lay still, holding his breath until he thought he could hold it no longer. At last the bear left, totally fooled by the Eskimo's brave performance.

Where did Nanook go? The disappointed bear wasn't hungry for long. It walked out of sight and encountered the Eskimo's friend as he hunted across the Arctic's frozen whiteness. The great Nanook killed and ate this other man, leaving the brave hunter to return to his village with the tale. For many years his people told the story of the hunter who outwitted Nanook at the bear's deadly game.

Bibliography
Volume I

Alter, J. Cecil. *Jim Bridger.* Norman, Oklahoma: University of Oklahoma Press, 1962.

Amundsen, Roald. *My Life As An Explorer.* New York: Doubleday, 1927.

Anonymous. *A Bear Fight in Arizona.* Army and Navy Journal. 1871.

Blevins, Winfred. *Give Your Heart to the Hawks.* New York: Avon Books, 1973.

Brown, David E. *The Grizzly of the Southwest.* Norman, Oklahoma: University of Oklahoma Press, 1985.
   —*The Last Grizzly.* Edited by John A. Murray. Tucson, Arizona: The University of Arizona Press, 1988.

Brown, Gary. *The Great Bear Almanac.* New York: Lyons and Burford, 1993.

Caras, Roger. *Monarch of Deadman Bay: The Life and Death of a Kodiak Bear.* Boston,

Massachussetts: Little, Brown, and Company, 1969.

Clark, Ella. *Indian Legends from the Northern Rockies.* Norman, Oklahoma: University of Oklahoma Press, 1966.

Clark, William and Meriwether Lewis. *Original Journals of the Lewis and Clark Expedition.* Edited by Reuben Gold Thwaites. New York: Dodd, Mead and Company, 1904-5.

Cleaveland, Agnes Morley. *No Life for a Lady.* Lincoln, Nebraska: University of Nebraska Press, 1977.

Clyman, James. *James Clyman, American Frontiersman.* Portland, Oregon: 1960.

Conrad, H. L. *Uncle Dick Wootton: The Pioneer Frontiersman of the Rocky Mountain Region.* Chicago, Illinois: W. E. Dibble and Co., 1890.

The Pioneers. Edited by George Constable. New York: Time-Life Books, 1974.

Cornwall, I. W. *Prehistoric Animals and Their Hunters.* New York: Frederick A. Praeger, 1968.

Cousins, Paul M. *Joel Chandler Harris: A Biography.* Baton Rouge, Louisiana: Louisiana State University Press, 1968.

Coyners, David H. *The Lost Trappers: A Collection of Interesting Scenes and Events in the Rocky Mountains.* Cincinnati, Ohio: J. A. and U. P. James, 1847.

Craighead Jr., Frank C. *Track of the Grizzly.* San Francisco, California: Sierra Publishing, 1979.

Cramond, Mike. *Killer Bears.* New York: Book Division, Times Mirror Magazines, 1981.

Fair, Jeff. *The Great American Bear:* Minocqua, Wisconsin: NorthWord Press, Inc., 1990.

Faulkner, William. "The Bear," in *Three Famous Short Novels* by William Faulkner. New York: Vintage Books, 1961.

Feazel, Charles T. *White Bear: Encounters with the Master of the Arctic Ice.* New York: Henry Holt and Company, 1990.

The Frontiersmen. Edited by Thomas H. Flaherty. The Old West Series. New York: Time-Life Books, 1977.

Fowler, Jacob. *The Journal of Jacob Fowler: Narrating an Adventure from Arkansas through the Indian Territory, Oklahoma, Kansas, Colorado, and New Mexico to the Sources of the Rio Grande Del Norte, 1921-1922.* Edited by Elliot Coues. New York: Francis P. Harper, 1898.

Mountain Men and Fur Traders of the Far West. Edited by Leroy Hafen. Glendale, California: Arthur H. Clark Co., 1965-72.

Herrero, Stephen. *Bear Attacks: Their Causes and Avoidance.* New York: Lyons and Burford, 1985.

Hittell, T. H. *The Adventures of James Capen Adams, Mountaineer and Grizzly Bear Hunter, of California.* New York: Charles Scribner's Sons, 1911.

Hornaday, William T. "A Fracas with Grizzly Bears." *Cosmopolitan.* Vol. 3, 1887.
—*Camp-Fires in the Canadian Rockies.* New York: Charles Scribner's Sons, 1904.

Irving, Washington. *Astoria: Anecdotes of an Enterprise Beyond the Rocky Mountains.* Philadelphia, Pennsylvania: Carey, Lea, and Blanchard, 1836.

Jackson, Donald. *Letters of the Lewis and Clark Expedition.* Urbana, Illinois: University of Illinois Press, 1962.

The Journals of Zebulon Montgomery Pike: With letters and related documents. Norman, Oklahoma: University of Oklahoma Press, 1966.

Kaniut, Larry. *Alaska Bear Tales.* Bothell, Washington: Alaska Northwest Books, 1983.
—*More Alaska Bear Tales.* Bothell, Washington: Alaska Northwest Books, 1989.

Kelsey, Henry. *The Kelsey Papers.* Ottawa, Ontario, Canada: Public Archives of Canada and the Public Record Office of Northern Ireland, 1929.

Kurten, Bjorn. *The Cave Bear Story: Life and Death of a Vanished Animal.* New York: Columbia University Press, 1976.

Laycock, George. *The Mountain Men.* New York: Outdoor Life Books, Sedgewood Press, 1988.

Leonard, Zenas. *Adventures of a Mountain Man: The Narrative of Zenas Leonard.* R. R. Donnelly and Sons, 1934.

Leopold, Aldo. *A Sand County Almanac.* Oxford: Oxford University Press, 1953.

Levitt, I. M., and Roy K. Marshall. *Star Maps for Beginners.* New York: Simon and Schuster, 1992.

Lynch, Wayne. *Bears: Monarchs of the Northern Wilderness.* Seattle, Washington: The Mountaineers, 1993.

McFarland, Elizabeth. *Wilderness of the Gila.* Albuquerque, New Mexico: University of New Mexico Press, 1974.

Mills, Enos. *The Grizzly, Our Greatest Wild Animal.* Boston, Massachusetts: Houghton Mifflin Company, 1919.

—*Wild Animal Homesteads.* Boston: Houghton Mifflin Company, 1932.

—*Wild Life on the Rockies.* Boston, Massachusetts: Houghton Mifflin Company, 1909.

Mills, William. *Bears and Men: A Gathering.* Chapel Hill, North Carolina: Algonquin Books of Chapel Hill, 1986.

Morgan, Dale L. *Jedediah Smith and the Opening of the West.* Lincoln, Nebraska: University of Nebraska Press, 1953.

Morison, Elting. *The History of Theodore Roosevelt.* Cambridge, Massachusetts: Harvard University Press, 1951-1954.

Murie, Adolph. *A Naturalist in Alaska.* New York: The Devin-Adair Co., 1961.

Norman, Howard. *Northern Tales: Traditional Stories of Eskimo and Indian Peoples.* New York: Pantheon Books, 1990.

O'Connor, Jack. *The Big Game Animals of North America.* New York: E. P. Dutton and Co., Inc., 1961.

Olsen, Jack. *Night of the Grizzlies.* New York: G. P. Putnam's Sons, 1969.

Ortega y Gasset, Jose. *Meditations on Hunting.* Translated by Howard B. Westcoll. New York: Scribners, 1972.

Rasky, Frank. *The Polar Voyagers: Explorers of the North.* Toronto, Ontario: McGraw-Hill Ryerson Ltd., 1976.

Ridpath, Ian. *The Monthly Sky Guide.* Kettering, United Kingdom: Cambridge University Press, 1987.

Rockwell, David. *Giving Voice to Bear.* Niwot, Colorado: Roberts Rinehart, 1991.

Roosevelt, Theodore. *Hunting Trips of a Ranchman.* New York: G. P. Putnam's Sons, 1885.

—*The Wilderness Hunter.* New York: G. P. Putnam's Sons, 1893.

—*The Works of Theodore Roosevelt.* Elkhorn Edition. New York: G. P. Putman's Sons, 1893.

—*The Youth's Companion.* New York: G. P. Putnam's Sons, 1893.

—"In the Louisiana Canebrakes." *Scribner's.* January 1908.

Russell, Andy. *Grizzly Country.* New York: Alfred A. Knopf, 1973.

Russell, Osborne. *Journal of a Trapper.* Edited by Aubrey L. Haines. Lincoln, Nebraska: University of Nebraska Press, 1986.

Ruxton, George Frederick. *Life in the Far West.* New York: Harper and Brothers, 1849.

Sandburg, Carl. *Abraham Lincoln: The Prairie Years.* Vol. 1, New York: Charles Scribner's Sons, 1948.

Schullery, Paul. *American Bears: Selections from the Writings of Theodore Roosevelt.* Boulder, Colorado: Colorado Associated University Press, 1983.

—*The Bear Hunter's Century.* New York: Dodd, Mead, and Company, Inc., 1988.

Sell, Henry Blackman and Victor Weybright. *Buffalo Bill and the Wild West.* Basin, Wyoming: Big Horn Books, 1979.

Shepard, Paul and Barry Sanders. *The Sacred Paw: The Bear in Nature, Myth, and Literature.* New York: Viking Penguin Inc., 1985.

Sparano, Vin T. *The Greatest Hunting Stories Ever Told.* New York: Beaufort Books, 1983.

Speck, Gordon. *Samuel Hearne and the Northwest Passage.* Caldwell, Idaho: Caxton Printers, Ltd., 1963.

Stevens, Montague. *Meet Mr. Grizzly: A Saga on the Passing of the Grizzly.* Albuquerque, New Mexico: University of New Mexico Press, 1943.

Stirling, Ian. *The Polar Bear.* The University of Michigan Press, 1988.

Storer, Traci I. and Lloyd P. Tevis, Jr. *California Grizzly.* Lincoln, Nebraska: University of Nebraska Press, 1955.

Sullivan, M. S. *The Travels of Jedediah Smith.* Santa Ana, California: Fine Arts Press, 1934.

Taylor, Colin F., editorial consultant. *Native American Myths and Legends.* New York: Smithmark Publishers, 1994.

Thomas, Alfred Barnaby. *After Coronado.* Norman, Oklahoma: University of Oklahoma Press, 1935.

Thompson, Albert E. *Those Early Days . . . Oldtimers' Memoirs.* Sedona, Arizona: Sedona Westerners, 1968.

Thornton, J. Q. *Oregon and California in 1848.* Vol. 2. New York, 1855.

Vestal, Stanley. *Jim Bridger, Mountain Man.* Lincoln, Nebraska: University of Nebraska Press, 1946.

Victor, Frances Fuller. *The River of the West*. Hartford, Connecticut: R. W. Bliss, 1870.

Wiseman, Ed. "Bear Attack." *Outdoor Life*, January, 1980.

Woodhead, Henry, editor. *The Spirit World*. The American Indian Series, New York: Time-Life Books, 1992.

Young, F. M., gathered by; edited by Coralie Beyers. *Man Meets Grizzly: Encounters in the Wild from Lewis and Clark to Modern Times*. Boston: Houghton Mifflin Co., 1980.

Yount, George C. "Chronicle of George Yount." Edited by Charles L. Camp, *California Historical Quar terly*, April, 1923.

❖ ❖ ❖

SCIENTIFIC PAPERS

Baur, Donald C. "Reconciling the Legal Mechanisms to Protect and Manage Polar Bears Under United States Laws and the Agreement for the Conservation of Polar Bears." Prepared for the Marine Mammal Commission, 1993.

Beattie, J. B. "Human-Brown Bear Interactions at Katmai National Park and Reserve." Sixth International Conference on Bear Research and Management, 1983.

Cushing, B. S. "The Effects of Human Menstruation on the Polar Bear." Madison, Wisconsin: Fifth International Conference on Bear Research and Management, 1980.

Gunther, Kerry A. "Bears and Menstruating Women." Information Paper BMO-7, Bear Management Office, Yellowstone National Park,1994.

Hunt, Carrie L. "Behavioral Responses of Bears to Tests of Repellents, Deterrents, and Aversive Condition ing." Master's thesis, University of Montana, 1984.

Jope, K. L. McArthur. "Implications of Habituation for Hikers in Grizzly Bear Habitat" (Abstract only). Sixth International Conference on Bear Research and Management, 1983. and Management, 1983.

Kendall, K.C. "Trends in grizzly-human confrontations, Glacier National Park" (Abstract only). Sixth International Conference on Bear Research and Management, 1983.

McCracken, Catherine, Debra A. Rose, and Kurt A. Johnson. "Status, Management, and Commercialization of the American Black Bear (Ursus americanus)." Published in cooperation with World Wildlife Fund, U.S.: World Wildlife Fund, Canada, January 1995.

"Bears: Their Biology and Management." Edited by C. J. Martinka and K. L. McArthur. Washington, D.C., U.S. Government Printing Office, 1980.

Middaugh, John P. "Human Injury from Bear Attacks in Alaska, 1900-1985." Alaska Medicine 29, No. 4 (1987).

Rogers, Lynn. "Social relationships, movements and population dynamics of black bears in northeastern Minnesota." Ph.D.disertation, University of Minnesota, 1977.

Schliebe, Scott L. "Conservation Plan for the Polar Bear in Alaska." U.S. Fish and Wildlife Service, Marine Mammals Management, Anchorage, Alaska, 1994.

Stenhouse, G.B. "Bear Detection and Deterrent Research Program: A Summary." Government of the Northwest Territories' Wildlife Services Department of Renewable Resources, 1983.